D0953715

The Great Hound Match of 1905

THE GREAT HOUND MATCH
OF 1905

*Alexander Henry Higginson, Harry Worcester Smith, and
the Rise of Virginia Hunt Country*

MARTHA WOLFE

Guilford, Connecticut

An imprint of Rowman & Littlefield

Distributed by NATIONAL BOOK NETWORK

Copyright © 2016 by Martha Wolfe

All rights reserved. No part of this book may be reproduced in any form or by any electronic or mechanical means, including information storage and retrieval systems, without written permission from the publisher, except by a reviewer who may quote passages in a review.

British Library Cataloguing in Publication Information Available

Library of Congress Cataloging-in-Publication Data Available

ISBN 978-1-58667-153-2 (hardcover)
ISBN 978-1-58667-154-9 (e-book)

∞™ The paper used in this publication meets the minimum requirements of American National Standard for Information Sciences—Permanence of Paper for Printed Library Materials, ANSI/ NISO Z39.48-1992.

Contents

To Betty K. and Robert L. Wolfe

Preface and Acknowledgments

In these pages you will find the story of a seemingly inconsequential event in the history of the United States of America, but a pivotal one for two gentlemen and a nearly forgotten town: Alexander Henry Higginson (1876–1958), Harry Worcester Smith (1865–1945) and Middleburg, Virginia. I have attempted to place The Great Hound Match of 1905 within the context of America's coming of age; the dawning of her first century as a world power; of America's emerging self-perception; her incipient popular cultural and of outdoor sporting events at the turn of the twentieth century, specifically that of foxhunting in America, which was only just finding an enthusiastic patronage with enough money to indulge in the sport in 1905. The Great Hound Match reflected the disparity of wealth in the still agrarian South as compared to the industrial North, as well as the changing self-images of America and Great Britain. The Match is also responsible for the existence, the essence, the mystique and the aura of Virginia's Hunt Country. Jacques Barzun, the American historian of ideas and philosopher of education, said that historical narrative should include "the range and wildness of individuality, the pivotal forces of trifles, the manifestations of greatness, the failures of unquestioned talent."[1] Concerning Harry Worcester Smith, Alexander Henry Higginson, and their Great Hound Match of 1905, I hope that I have fulfilled Mr. Barzun's challenge.

Much has been written about The Match. If you are a foxhunter you may have heard of it, especially if you live in Virginia, where it took place, or in Massachusetts, where the competitors lived. With the coming of the one hundred tenth anniversary of The Match, I hope you will find it historically, scientifically, and culturally interesting. I am not a trained historian nor am I a philosopher; I am a storyteller. Forgive me if you sense some embellishment: I was raised among hypochondriacs and hyperbolic hysterics. Though I am wary of psycho-biography, I might presume too much from a person's actions, including the men I write about here. And, I'm not especially interested in *the* Truth, for what is Truth but perspective?

This book is a castle of sugar cubes. There are eight foundation chapters of straight nonfiction material covering—in a journalistic vein—events, trends, fads, discoveries, and vagaries that were popular and prescient at the turn of the twentieth century. Attached to the foundation with a fragile mortar of creative nonfiction, a sort of sugar coating, are the blocks that represent Story: nine chapters written from the point of view of an omniscient narrator who was there. With a little imagination—the ability to suspend disbelief for just a little while—the sugar castle will stand; doubt and it will fall. Of course, no one is alive today who experienced The Great Hound Match of 1905, but there are so many accounts, particularly Allen Potts's wonderful write-ups in the *Richmond Times Dispatch* available through the Library of Congress's Chronicling America website (http://chroniclingamerica.loc .gov/lccn/sn85038615/1905-11-01/ed-1/seq-1/) and other books and articles, available principally through the National Sporting Library & Museum in Middleburg, Virginia, that a narrative of virtually every moment of those two weeks in November of 1905 can be creditably represented.

I wish to thank the National Sporting Library & Museum (NSLM) for granting me a John H. Daniels Fellowship, during which I conducted the initial research of this book. Thank you Rick Stoutamyer, Lisa Campbell, Mickey Gustafson, and John Connolly, the library's George L. Ohrstrom Jr. Librarian, for your careful stewardship and guidance through the Harry Worcester Smith and Alexander Henry Higginson Archives, as well as the library's incredible rare books and general collections. Thanks to the library's executive director, Melanie Mathews, and the George L. Ohrstrom Curator, Claudia Pheiffer, for your support and friendship during my long hours in the basement. Thanks also to the staff of the American Antiquarian Society in Worcester, Massachusetts; to that of the Worcester Public Library; to Robyn Christensen at the Worcester Historical Museum, and to Molly Bruce, archivist at Worcester Polytechnic Institute's Gordon Library. Thanks to the staff at the Library of London for access to their Alexander Henry Higginson Collection.

Thank you, Jed Lyons, President and CEO of Rowman and Littlefield, for taking a chance on this, my first book. Thanks to Keith Wallman, Holly Rubino, Lynn Zelem, and Jessica Plaskett at Lyons Press for their attention to detail during its publication.

I wish also to thank my friend, colleague, and fellow foxhunter Norm Fine, editor of Derrydale Press's Foxhunting Library, for his friendship and guidance, and to his friends, and now mine, Kerry and John Glass of Lincoln, Massachusetts, for their thoughts, brainstorms, insights, and tips about foxhunting in general and The Match specifically. Thank you, Kerry, for introducing me to Mr. Albert Poe, former huntsman for the Piedmont Hounds and the Middleburg and Fairfax Hunts. Thank you, Mr. Poe, for spending that day in October 2014, educating this novice about the intricacies of a huntsman's talent, intuition, fortitude, and brains. Thanks to Guy Allman, huntsman for Blue Ridge Hunt, for your insight into your profession. Thank you to Kitty Smith, who kindly told me her family stories about her grandfather. Thank you, Nat and Sherry Morison, for your hospitality at Welbourne, the Dulany family home. And thank you to the Bonnie family for allowing me to visit Oakley.

Thanks to my equestrian friends Doris Stimpson, former MFH of Blue Ridge Hunt, who read much of this narrative and provided insight to a Master's role. Thanks Terry Trimble-Catlett, Cathy Frederickson, Linda Roberts, Marillyn Davis, and Lynn Hottel for riding with me and listening to my stories as I fleshed them out. And, as always, to my great and good friend, Patsy Davis, for listening as I droned on. Thanks to my writing friends who gave valuable feedback, Sharon Hicks-Bartlett, Lydia Strohl, Howard Means, Brenda Waugh, and especially to my children, Calvin, Duncan, and Robert Shabb, and to my sister, Peggy McKee, for listening to me perseverate for the last year. Thanks to my teachers, friends, and colleagues at Bennington Writing Seminars for their enormous efforts and support, most especially Susan Cheever, who convinced me that foxhunting is a worthy subject about which to write.

And most especially thank you, Bill, for living with me and loving me, no matter what.

1

The Crowning Point of All

STORYTELLERS CLAIM THAT THERE IS REALLY ONLY ONE STORY IN THE world: "A Stranger Comes to Town." In this case, two strangers came to two towns in Virginia, bringing with them their separate entourages—private trainloads of friends and their horses, trunks of tack, boots, formal and informal clothing, food and wine, servants, and of course their hound dogs. Neither Middleburg nor Upperville, Virginia, had seen the likes since J. E. B. Stuart established his headquarters at the Beverage House (now the Red Fox Inn) in Middleburg during the Gettysburg Campaign. Alexander Henry Higginson of South Lincoln and Harry Worcester Smith of Grafton, Massachusetts, had determined that the Loudoun Valley in Virginia's pastoral Piedmont was the best place to prove the relative worth of their chosen foxhounds.

It was November of 1905, the peak of foxhunting season across the Midlands of England and up and down the east coast of North America, and these folks had come south from already snow-covered New England to the relatively mild winter in Virginia to hunt her plentiful red foxes. There was to be a contest, a Great Hound Match, between two packs of foxhounds—one English and one American. The English hounds carried, on their great stout forearms and deep chests, the monumental weight of centuries of foxhunting in England and were expected to make their hound dog ancestors proud of their New World conquest. The American hounds were expected to show those stodgy old Brits how it was done over here—with spunk and intuition, individuality, drive, and nerve. Of course the dogs just wanted to chase a fox or two; it was their Masters who loaded the poor hounds and The Match, this moment in history, with the weighty question of worth.

Englishmen and women had been hunting foxes on horseback for a couple of centuries by the turn of the twentieth century, but in America foxhunting was only just finding a following among its newly gilded millionaires now that the second industrial revolution had established a landed and leisure class, particularly in the North. "Enthusiasm for the sport literally swept the country as the century mark approached. . . . If ever an era was golden in any country, it was this era in America."[1]

The proverbial spark that struck The Match came in the form of a letter to the editors of *Rider and Driver* dated January 21, 1905, from Harry Worcester Smith, a self-made millionaire, owner and operator of a cotton manufacturing plant in booming Worcester, Massachusetts, who liked to say that he did everything, he *lived*, "For the Sake of Sport in America." Smith's letter stated his dual intentions: first to ask his venerable old hunting club, the "Brunswick Fur Club" based in Brunswick, Maine, to change its name to the "Brunswick Foxhound Club"; and second to have the club adopt a new standard for the American foxhound. The significance of the first was to change the public's perception of the club from one of trapping and shooting defenseless animals to that of a prestigious club of foxhunters, specifically those who did so from the back of a horse with a pack of hounds. If the Brunswick Foxhound Club were to adopt a new standard and press the American Kennel Club to do so, the impact of the second rule change would be to officially recognize the American foxhound, distinct from pure and half-bred imported hounds from England, making it possible for hounds bred and raised in America to compete against one another in field and bench trials rather than against their very different cousins from across the way.

In his letter to *Rider and Driver* Harry Worcester Smith advocated "a new standard for the American foxhound." He believed that the smaller-boned, leaner, tougher Southern hound bred for running the Appalachian foothills was better than the larger, bigger-boned English hound at finding and killing American foxes, "which is the crowning point of all." Smith never imagined small things; his efforts were usually universal, practically biblical. His goal, beginning in 1904, was to establish an American foxhound that could chase the Brits from American soil once and for all.

The editors printed (coincidentally?) in that same issue a letter from Alexander Henry Higginson telling the sporting world at large that he had recently received a draft of hounds from England and claiming that they would clearly benefit not only his own hunting, but that of all of North America, due to their excellent lineage. A friend of Higginson's, Julian Ingersoll Chamberlain, using the nom de plume "Lincoln," also wrote a letter reiterating Higginson's confidence, saying that Middlesex Hunt's new stallion hound "Visitor" (1899) by the Milton "Redcar" (1890) out of Belvoir "Vigilance" (1895) had all the qualities "essential to prevent the tendency of thoroughbred English hounds to deteriorate in bone after a few generations in America." "Lincoln" went on to label the "so-called American hound . . . weedy and chance-bred."

Here were A. Henry Higginson and his friend "Lincoln," deriding the very thing that Harry Worcester Smith believed was the key to great sport in America. Smith had many friends in Fauquier and Loudoun Counties in Virginia, where he had been invited to hunt, beginning in 1889, with the Dulany family in Upperville. With the help of Burrell Frank Bywaters, a hound breeder in Warrenton, Virginia, Smith had begun to assemble a pack of American-bred hounds that he believed would be able to run down and kill the red fox that had so far, in his opinion, eluded the British imports. When he read Higginson's and Lincoln's opinion of his championed hound, he must have spit his soup.

What better way to sell a newspaper? The editors of *Rider and Driver* essentially acted as seconds in the duel of words that ensued the winter of 1904 and through the spring of 1905 between Smith and Higginson:

Higginson: "The truth of the matter is, there *is* no *American* foxhound to-day."

Smith: "That those who have only in the past twenty-four months graduated from hunting foot beagles, still believe in the English hounds, I am not surprised."

Lincoln: "Surely if we cherish fond hopes of a future standard for the foxhound in America, we shall not, as sensible men breed to this type."

Smith: "As he is a member of the Middlesex Hunt Club, I refuse to converse with 'Lincoln' further."

Higginson: "What Mr. Smith wants, what we all want, is a hound that will kill foxes in America. How to get it? Mr. Smith suggests turning to a lighter hound. Why not take the English standard?"

Smith: "The English breeders are the best in the world, and they have produced a type which is without a doubt absolutely satisfactory for use in their own country, but when they cannot show sport here, as Graham [Joseph A., author of *The Sporting Dog*] puts it, 'they drop into the discard.'"

Within weeks—two weeks of bickering, chest pounding, false modesty, and outright bragging from both camps—Higginson writes, "Finally I am ready to make an offer:

"Let Mr. Smith choose a judge, let me choose a judge, let the two name a third.

"Then let Mr. Smith go to any fair fox-hunting country in America with such hounds as he chooses—and I will bring such clean-bred hounds as I choose and my huntsman and whippers-in—and we'll hunt on alternate days for love, money, or marbles. Then if his hounds kill more foxes than mine or show better sport, I'll admit I'm wrong—but not until then."

Throughout the summer, north and south and back and forth across "the puddle," debate raged and the respective camps swelled. *The Washington Post*, *The New York Herald*, *The New York Post*, *The Boston Herald*, *The Boston Evening Transcript*, *The Baltimore Sun*, *The Richmond Times Dispatch*, and *The London Times* kept a running commentary. Basil Nightingale of Leamington, England, wrote to the *New York Post*:

"American hounds were hunted in this neighborhood with the Blackmore Vale. At a check their curious deep note could be heard in the distance coming nearer and nearer. They had enormous ears, as long as bloodhounds', short coupled, compact bodies, were very light of bone, shocking legs and feet, and were quite incapable as regards pace and power of crossing a country with English hounds. They were tailed off directly. It's nice to think of them when one gets low."

By August the Piedmont Valley of Virginia was chosen as the site and each competitor agreed to put down $1000—winner take all. *Rider and Driver*'s editors agreed to hold the cash prize for the winner, but a hitch stalled their giddy-up when in July Higginson neglected to send his first installment of $250. Smith, ever the testy little fellow, withdrew his money, writing to Higginson via *Rider and Driver*, "I regret exceedingly that you have not taken this matter more seriously." Higginson complied forthwith.

The hounds that Mr. Higginson so adamantly championed were bred in the heart of England's Midlands. Smith had bred his own hounds from stock he had purchased in Virginia and Kentucky. Where Smith's hounds were prized for their unmistakable musical cry, individuality, and hard-driving attitude, with or without their pack mates, English hounds were known for their pliability, their obedience, and their willingness to stay together and hunt as a pack. For Higginson, the rub was Smith's lack of respect for Tradition and the foxhound's English heritage. "The usual Virginia pack," he writes much later in his 1931 autobiography *Try Back*, "consisted in those days of six or seven couples of scrawny, ill-kept hounds, *coupled together* (scandalous) and looking for all the world as if they'd never had a square meal." He's referring here to the custom of using a double collar to literally tie two hounds together, usually an older hound with a younger one, to keep them from taking off on their own, a habit that the American hound breeders were actually proud of. Higginson respected, above all, the English hounds' proclivity to be led in their every movement by their huntsman.

The differences between Smith's and Higginson's personalities were as distinct as—and one could even say mirrored—that of their hounds. If Higginson was a prig, Smith was a scalawag; if Higginson was a Brahman, Smith was of the working class; if Higginson was a purebred, Smith was a mutt. Higginson's roots were deeply puritanical; Smith's were Catholic in religion and catholic in taste.

While Higginson had made the challenge and appeared serious about it, Smith managed to turn the coming Match into a moral quest for America's absolution from Britain's tyranny (again). At times the real question, which hounds could hunt best, got mixed up in a patriotic brouhaha. F. S. Peer, author and hound man, wrote to *Rider and Driver* to remind their readers of the "absurdity of making the question one of pseudo-patriotism."[2] Others pointed out that the differences in foxhunting in America and England, the terrain, the climate and relative humidity, and thus the scientific aspects of scent, the very nature of the fox—some said England's foxes were basically domesticated—made the very question somewhat ridiculous. But once the challenge was made, nobody was willing to back down, least of all Smith or Higginson.

In January of 1905 Teddy Roosevelt took the Oval Office in his first elected term and "The Scarlet Pimpernel" opened in London. In February, the same month The Match was made, the Russo-Japanese War, the twentieth century's first Great War, ended. That March Mata Hari (her name means "eye of the day") was introduced in Paris and Teddy Roosevelt took the Oval Office in his first elected term. In May 110 acres in the middle of the Nevada desert were auctioned and Las Vegas was founded. Early in June the first motor lorry ran between London and Brighton and later that month the Automobile Association was inaugurated in England. That October the HMS *Dreadnaught* was laid down (to be launched the following February) and the Wright Flyer III stayed aloft for a full thirty minutes. Mark Twain's characters Huckleberry Finn and Tom Sawyer were banned at the Brooklyn Public Library for their "coarseness, deceitful and mischievousness" behavior.[3] On October 31 six men met at the Piedmont Inn in Upperville, Virginia, to formalize the beginning of The Great Hound Match of 1905.

2

Meeting at Piedmont Inn

Upperville, Virginia
Three o'clock p.m., Tuesday, October 31, 1905

*"The eyes of the hunting world are upon [Higginson and Smith], and
true sportsmen are willing to place the laurels where they are honestly
won whether it be by the foxhounds of England or America."*
—J. M. HENRY, *RICHMOND TIMES-DISPATCH*, NOVEMBER 1, 1905

THE MEN AT THE TABLE, SIX RUDDY-CHEEKED, BEWHISKERED, AND CLEAN-
shaven blokes, struggled to look official. "Whiskeys all around," Jim Maddux, one of the judges, said to a waiter in a grubby apron who appeared
in the doorway.

"Not for me," Harry Worcester Smith said.

"Doubles for the judges," Alexander Henry Higginson said.

Another judge, Dr. Charles McEachran, said, "A toast: to The Match,"
and they all stood.

"To The Match!"

There was talk of the weather; the weather is uppermost in every hunting man's mind. There was talk of recent accidents resulting in sprained
and broken body parts and horses out of action. Finally Mr. Movius, the
judge from Philadelphia said, "Shall we get down to business then?"

Alexander Henry Higginson—his friends called him "Hig"—winced
as he crossed his leg beneath the table. He was twenty-nine and built
like a welterweight—stocky, densely muscled, not especially agile, but
strong and solid. Harry Worcester Smith—his friends called him Harry
Worcester Smith—spread his knees, leaned back, and ran a well-tanned

and gnarled hand through his thick curly hair. Twelve years his opponent's senior, Smith stood five-foot-seven, fit as a jockey; he was confident, perhaps overconfident. Higginson looked at his fingernails and
winced again.

"Anything wrong?" Smith asked Higginson, knowing full well that
Higginson had two broken ribs and a busted knee.

"Nothing," Higginson replied.

The others at the table looked at one another, almost expecting
a fistfight to break out; the tension was palpable. Smith and Higginson had each chosen a judge and together they chose another more or
less impartial judge. Smith had chosen Jim Maddux, Master of nearby
Warrenton Hunt, while Higginson had chosen Charles McEachran,
Master of Montreal's Hunt. The third judge, Hal Movius, Master of
the Brandywine Hunt, had come down from Philly. Allen Potts, who
hunted in Richmond with the Keswick and Deep Run Hunts and was
a reporter for the *Richmond Times Dispatch*, had agreed to act as clerk
and scribe.

"How is your brother?" Dr. McEachran asked Smith.

"Oh, he's fine," Smith said. "Broke his collarbone, is all. He'll be riding by the end of the week. That is if I have anything to do with it."

"Mr. Higginson, how many couple of hounds will you be hunting for
the duration of this Match?" Allen Potts asked.

"Eighteen and a half," Higginson said. Smith snorted.

"Smith?" Potts asked.

"Six and a half."

Higginson raised an eyebrow. His thirty-seven hounds against Smith's
thirteen. This was going to be easy.

"Before we proceed," Smith said, "I'd like to offer Mr. Higginson
the first day's sport." They had agreed to hunt on alternate days for two
full weeks beginning on Wednesday, November 1, with both intervening
Sundays as rest days.

All eyes on Higginson. "Most sporting of you, thank you. I should
like to meet at Welbourne."

"And might I suggest that you draw the covert at Beaverdam Creek
first?"

8

"I'll take that into consideration," Higginson said. He had no idea to where Mr. Smith might be referring, but all the country thereabouts looked fine. "Why not?"

"Why not, indeed?" Smith said. Higginson wished that Smith's eyes didn't twinkle quite so brightly. The room seemed dim and small. The hotel was a shabby affair with wooden chairs and tables. A dismal little fire lit one end of the room. A few old gas lamps lit the rest. The town didn't even have electricity yet. Higginson felt he had stepped back at least fifty years. He was tired and sore. The train ride from New York had been endless, though the company was good. All of his best hunting friends had come along for the sport, bringing with them strings of horses, tack, and chests of necessities, including food and wine of course, for who knew what was available in the backwoods of Virginia? First Philly and then Washington, then deeper and deeper into the countryside behind a decrepit steam engine belching soot and stopping every five miles until it reached The Plains, a crossroads with nothing but the station and a post office combined. A crowd of Virginians, most very friendly, but some, practically jeering, had come to see the Yankees. Then a buggy ride in the dark over roads that should not be called roads—dirt tracks, pitted footpaths was more appropriate. Luckily his servant, Cotesworth, had brought his runabout and his best pony, Six Bits, to the station, and she could navigate anything at any time in any weather. Well, at least the bourbon was good.

"What time will you move off, Mr. Higginson?" Potts asked, pencil in hand.

A horse whinnied outside on the only street in town. Buggies lined either side of the front door. Through the window Higginson watched a groom put a blanket on a pretty sorrel saddle horse; the sun was dropping. A one-horse town if there ever was one, Higginson thought. "Oh, shall we say, seven?" he asked the room at large.

"The sun will have been up an hour by then," Smith said.

"Actually it rises at six thirty-six tomorrow," Potts said. Smith slumped, crossed his arms and looked out the window.

"Let's make it six forty-five then," Higginson said.

"The earlier the better, I always say," was Smith's retort. "I suppose the Middlesex will be all in pink?"

"I won't be following tomorrow," Higginson said. He had decided on the way to the meeting not to ride on the first day. He would wrap his ribs and take a day to recuperate. He'd hoped that the first day's hunting would have been Smith's, but he couldn't very well refuse Smith's falsely magnanimous proffer of the first day's sport. "And we shan't be out past midday."

Smith's eyes twinkled even brighter. The fire lit a golden thread of hair at his temple.

"Of course, my huntsman, Cotesworth, will be dressed formally. It's a formal affair after all." Higginson straightened his stocky frame to relieve some pressure from his blasted ribs.

"I'll be following and I'll be damned if I'm wearing red," Smith said. "My staff and I will be in Grafton's grey and black, as usual. If those colors were good enough for John Peel, they're good enough for me."

"Of course," Higginson said. Of course Smith wouldn't wear scarlet. The man had no sense of tradition; if he'd had, The Match wouldn't even be taking place. American foxhounds indeed. There *is* no American fox-hound. The only true foxhound is, and always will be, English.

"And, by the way," Smith continued, "on Grafton's days we'll be out until sunset. Your hounds are used to hunting England's semi-domesticated fox in open country with chest-high scent. Mine can catch a wild fox's pad-scent set down yesterday, so we'll be out early and we'll stay out all day."

"Very well, gentleman," Potts interrupted. "Will you have guests, Mr. Higginson?"

"Yes," he said. "Here is a list. Five all together. Mrs. Pierce will be the Middlesex Hunt's Field Master tomorrow." As he passed the list, Higginson bumped his knee on the corner of the table and moaned.

"Too bad about that fall," Smith said to Higginson. "And did you win the race?"

"No," Higginson said. "I did not. It was the last steeplechase to be held at Morris Park's old race track, you know. A pity it is closing."

"Yeah, too bad."

"You're not racing anymore, are you?" Higginson asked Smith.

"Nope," Smith said, "and spare me your mock concern. You know damned well I've won every gentleman's steeplechase in the country. I am *the* gentleman rider in America, so I don't need to prove myself to the likes of you. I don't race anymore, I hunt foxes. My hounds race now and I follow their pace. Be warned, it's fast."

"And how many guests will be out with you tomorrow?" Potts asked Smith, trying to dispel the rising heat, but wherever Harry Worcester Smith was, there would be controversy, heated words, and sometimes punches thrown, so there was no need to even try.

"Zero," Smith said. "Just my staff. On Thursday I'll be Grafton's huntsman *and* Master. First whip will be Mal Richardson; second whip, Claude Hatcher, and Ham Jackson will scout for me."

"He's a Negro, is he not?" Higginson asked.

"Yes, Ham's a colored boy, and he knows this country better than anybody around," Smith said. "He was Hunter Dulany's huntsman for years. Believe it: he can ride better than any of us."

"It's like having another pack of hounds with you when you ride with Ham," Jim Maddux said.

"I'd like to make something official—in the minutes of this meeting, I mean," Smith said to Potts.

Here it comes, Higginson thought, some one thing or the other to change the rules yet again. The last eight months had been nothing but constant bantering back and forth in the mails and the news about rules, rules, rules.[1] *Rider and Driver* had made a great deal of money in subscriptions because of this Match. Their readership was up, and they'd succeeded in whipping this thing into a national phenom.

"I think we should extend a formal invitation across the mountain to the Blue Ridge Hunt, Mr. Edward Gay Butler and his guests, and also, let the minutes reflect that the first day's sport be dedicated to Colonel Richard H. Dulany. It is, after all, his land that we will be hunting across these next two weeks. He and his son and nephew have been Masters and huntsmen of the Piedmont Hounds for fifty years now, and it is due to their kind invitation that we are here."

"I understand you've been recently appointed Master of the Piedmont Hounds," Charles McEachran said to Smith. "You must know the country well already."

"I do," Smith said.

McEachran looked at Higginson, who returned a wide-eyed stare. This was news to him. Cotesworth had sent him a note saying that he didn't trust Smith, that Smith wasn't following "the spirit of The Match" and that he'd wished that they'd held the damn thing in the Genesee Valley. But it was too cold in upstate New York this time of year; they'd already stopped hunting up there. The scent, if any, would have been scant. No, Higginson was confident. His hounds were perfect. They'd only been in the States for three months, but they were damned fine hounds. *"The best lot of hounds America has ever seen,"* a *Boston Globe* reporter had said, and the paper had printed that very thing. They were a fine, upstanding lot and they were going to run these pathetic little "American" chance-bred mutts into the ground.

Smith sat back, knees spread, one stuttering to an inner motor that fired within the man. A tap on the window by a black hand waved him outside.

"Are we all agreed, then?" asked judge Movius.

Jim Maddux said, "One more thing to add. Something's come up and I will be absent Friday and Saturday of this week. I'd like to propose that Fred Okie take my place for those two days."

"I don't know this gentleman," Higginson said. "Where is he from?"

"Don't get your knickers in a twist, Higginson," Smith said. "He's from right here in Upperville. He'll be able to keep up, don't worry. I approve of the replacement."

"I'm not worried if he can keep up, he'll be acting as your judge, but why wasn't I informed of this until now?" Higginson said.

"I admit it's sudden," Maddux said. "I have hunting engagements elsewhere."

"Very well," Higginson said. "There's little we can do about it now." He felt as though he was being slowly, by tiny increments, denied a fair chance in this thing. With each passing day he abhorred Smith ever more—in his opinion the man was an absolute sod.

A motion was made and carried; the meeting adjourned. Higginson stood up slowly. McEachran went to speak in his ear. Smith vacated the room as quickly as he'd arrived. "Thanks, Ham," he said outside. "I hate a damn long-winded meeting. Let's go." He shoved his cap over his ears, vaulted aboard The Cad and took off east toward Oakley. The high winds forecast for the next day, Wednesday, had begun to stir. Thursday's forecast was fair. "We got Thursday, Ham," Smith called over the clatter of their horses' shoes. "That idiot Higginson hasn't even looked at the weather." Glancing back, he saw Higginson stepping into his waiting buggy.

3

America's Happy Fin de Siècle

"There is something in the close of that arbitrary division of time which we call a century that powerfully affects the human imagination, and through it the movements of society."[1]

AT FIRST GLANCE, 1905 DOESN'T SEEM SO SPECIAL. THE NEW CENTURY is well under way. A specific time or place rarely sees its historical significance; foresight is a luxury afforded to those with money and a warm bed.

It was a good year for Alexander Henry Higginson, Harry Worcester Smith, and most Americans. Progress was everywhere. We were coming of age, and like any young adult, we were full of ourselves—our potential. Higginson's father had built a new house for his only son, with new stables and grand kennels. Alexander Henry Higginson had established his hunt, become Master, hired his huntsman and staff, and acquired his hounds. He had a new pastime and money to devote to it. He must have felt he was climbing to the top of his game, experiencing the surge of confidence that comes with understanding the complexities of a new endeavor— a dream within sight. Smith had declared his mission: to establish the American foxhound as a new and unequaled breed.

Perhaps neither realized it, but their devotions and resolve mirrored their time—the push and pull, the struggle between American and European influences, was tremendous. "Modern" and "progressive" were the new norms. The bet, the gamble, the audacious, ludicrous wager that was The Great Hound Match was a sign of the times, a piece of the puzzle that became history. Thinking about 1905 a century hence comes with a proleptic tendency to pity the poor planet for what it was about to experience, but for Hig and Harry, the future was nothing but bright.

What was it about that time, the year 1905, that pushed Harry Worcester Smith to imagine something new, something that had never been recognized before, that had existed in some form, but had never been refined enough to declare itself *new*? And why was Alexander Henry Higginson so well convinced that the status quo was not only good enough, but better than it had ever been, could ever be? The German philosopher Georg Hegel, a century earlier, had observed that "no man can surpass his own time, for the spirit of his time [*der Geist seiner Zeit*] is also his own spirit.[2] Both men, in equal measure, embodied the spirit of their times.

Of course ordinary people rarely recognize the art or aesthetic period in which we live; most probably prefer something in the recent or distant past. Artists, musicians, philosophers, and scientists paint, compose, think about, and experiment with one another's material, the critics name what it is they've done, and we the people try to keep up. We react to what is made and thought, politicians react to our reactions, high brow meets low, and an epoch is born. At the turn of the twentieth century, in the midst of the second industrial revolution when the money, and the power that came with it, had crossed the Atlantic and gilded our borders, America was realizing her place on the planet. By 1905 the Gilded Age was ending; the Progressives were questioning the monopolists; the Socialists were challenging the Capitalists; positivists were up against anti-positivists who held intuition above empiricism; pluralism battled imperialism. Old aristocracies in Europe were threatened by the nouveau-riches in America. Pessimists called it the Fin de Siècle. Later, to Europeans looking back from the wreckage of two World Wars, it was known as the Belle Époque. 1905 was also an *Annus Mirabilis*, a "Miracle Year."

Following the worst depression the United States had yet seen, that of 1893, the country was in a self-congratulatory boom. U.S. Steel had recently become our first billion-dollar company. Between 1870 and 1900 the average real wage for a non-farm worker increased by more than 50 percent. Between 1897 and 1914 US overseas investments quadrupled from $634 million to $2.6 billion. Much like America is to China today, Europe was America's consumer market, and England was the capital of capital. Monopoly was more than a board game.[3] Besides U.S. Steel, there was International Harvester, Quaker Oats, American Tobacco, Standard Oil, Diamond Match, Kodak Camera, and Carnation Milk. DuPont made the world's gunpowder.

Here's how London journalist William T. Stead described the typical Englishman's morning around that time:

> *The Average man rises in the morning from his New England sheets, he shaves with Williams' soap and a Yankee safety razor, pulls on his Boston boots over his socks from North Carolina, fastens his Connecti-cut braces, slips his Waltham or Waterbury watch in his pocket, and sits down to breakfast. There he congratulates his wife on how her Illinois straightfront corset sets off her Massachusetts blouse, and he tackles his breakfast where he eats bread made from prairie flour (possibly doctored at the special establishments on the lakes), tinned oysters from Baltimore and a little Kansas City bacon, while his wife plays with a slice of Chicago ox-tongue. The children are given "Quaker" oats. At the same time he reads his morning paper printed by American machines, on American paper, with American ink, and possibly edited by a smart journalist from New York.[4]*

On March 4, 1905, Theodore Roosevelt, the man Henry Adams called "pure act," took hold of his second term as President of the United States, his first having been the result of McKinley's assassination just six months into his own second term. Teddy, elected in a landslide, enthu-siastically carried out his predecessor's Progressive policies and took his "square deal" to the people. The boom helped. Amusement parks with Ferris Wheels and roller coasters sprang up; William Phelps Eno con-ceived of the STOP sign—a two-foot by two-foot sheet of white metal with black lettering; dance madness took hold in dance halls; for the price of a nickel anyone could stay as long as she or he liked to watch a silent movie accompanied by live piano at a "Nickelodeon"; "basket ball" (later shortened to one word) took off in a YMCA in Albany, NY.

Americans Eva Tanguay and Trixie Friganza rode the Vaudeville cir-cuit along with Canadian May Irwin; ragtime thrived and, a little later, in answer to "blackface," jazz was born. Charles Ives wrote his Symphony No. 2, radically including American folk tunes, and in 1893 Antonín Dvořák wrote his Symphony No. 9 "From the New World" for the New York Philharmonic. By 1907 symphony orchestras had been established in Chicago, Cincinnati, Boston, Pittsburg, Philadelphia, Minneapolis, and St. Louis; in 1909 the New York Philharmonic reorganized and expanded.

Samuel Clemens (Mark Twain), Theodore Dreiser, Jack London, James Russell Lowell, William Dean Howells, Sinclair Lewis, Frank Norris, Stephen Crane, Sarah Orne Jewett, Kate Chopin, and Ellen Glasgow—all preceded by Walt Whitman of course—found their distinctive American voices around the turn of the twentieth century.

Artists Frederic Church and Albert Bierstadt were illuminating the Hudson River and the American West. A decade before the groundbreaking 1913 International Exhibition of Modern Art (the Armory Show) in New York City, Alfred Stieglitz introduced America to avant-garde at his "Little Galleries of the Photo-Secession," precursor to his famous studio "291" at that address on Fifth Avenue where the first American exhibitions of Modern Art took place. Works by Pamela Coleman Smith, Auguste Rodin's studio drawings, and modern works by Matisse, Cezanne, Picasso, Duchamp, and Marius de Zayas were exhibited. Exhibitions at "291" helped launch young American artists like Max Weber, John Marin, Arthur Dove, and Marsden Hartley. America's fin de siècle, as opposed to that of Europe, was fueled with a "moral fire" and her artists were "serious about life and its responsibilities."[5] Between 1879 and 1897 fin de siècle idealists in Chicago established the Art Institute of Chicago, Chicago Orchestra, University of Chicago, Field Museum, and the Newberry and Crerar Libraries.

Europe's mood was more pessimistic, filled with loathing for an embedded bourgeoisie. While Europe's fin de siècle meant revolution inspired by revulsion, in America, that empty place full of promise (population 83 million), fin de siècle meant a resistance to pessimism and high achievement was inspired by great art and architecture. Though John Singer Sargent had painted Isabelle Stewart Gardner "décolleté," by European standards her decadence was modest. Sarah Bernhardt and

Mata Hari embodied Old World vice as Europe's femmes fatales; Marcel Proust searched for Lost Time; Edmond Rostand's popular play *Cyrano de Bergerac* (1897) was still the rage; and Thomas Mann wrote about the German bourgeoisie in his epic novel *Buddenbrooks* (1901). The Polish expat Joseph Conrad settled in England to write his antiheroic early modern novels including *Heart of Darkness* (1899) and *Nostromo* (1904) alongside Rudyard Kipling, H. G. Wells, Irishman Bram Stoker, Arthur Conan Doyle, E. M. Forester, and Beatrix Potter. Germany was the center of philosophy and science while Paris, though still reeling from the Dreyfus Affair, was the aesthetic center of the Western world.

Edward VII, better known as Bertie (Rudyard Kipling called him "that corpulent voluptuary"), took his throne in England at the ripe old age of fifty-nine August 9, 1902. A proven playboy, he had affairs with many prominent women including Lillie Langtry, France's incomparable Sarah Bernhardt, and Jennie Jerome Churchill, mother of Winston and daughter of Leonard Jerome, the American boom-or-bust financier and thoroughbred enthusiast who helped found the American Jockey Club. Bertie partied with the Rothschilds and witnessed the end of Gladstone's half-century political career and the rise of his friend, the conservative Benjamin Disraeli. He disliked his nephew Kaiser Wilhelm II of Germany, who later blamed Edward's signing of the Triple Entente with France and Russia for the Great War. Bertie was on the throne when England came quickly and not so quietly out of her Victorian closet.

Then, as now, as always, people everywhere were experiencing a tug-of-war of confusing and conflicting forces from without and within, and nowhere were those forces better exhibited than at the more than fifty World's Fairs held between 1890 and 1905.

Ehrich Weiss, age nineteen, later known as Harry Houdini, got his start at the World's Columbian Exposition in Chicago in 1893, for which the magnificent Palace of Fine Arts, now the Museum of Science and Industry, was constructed. In Chicago "a young nation proclaimed a new dawn."[6] The Chicago World's Fair's anthem was "Not Matter but Mind; Not Things but Men," and Houdini made people believe that Mind over Matter was his method of escape. The fair's White City represented the American Myth of starting over, of reinventing itself again (and again, and again). Seven years later the century's turn was marked in Paris at The Exposition Universelle, for which the Eiffel Tower was built, where France's Herminie Cadolle first exhibited her *soutien-gorge*—the modern bra—and where American Frank D. Lewis won a gold medal for his ultra-large #20 fountain pen.

Then, in 1904, the St. Louis World's Fair was held to commemorate the one hundredth anniversary of the Louisiana Purchase. The fair's publicity brochure called it "The Greatest of Expositions." West of the city in Forest Park on what is now Washington University's campus, the twelve-hundred-acre site was designed by German-born landscape architect and city planner George Kessler, a member of the City Beautiful movement that had begun with the Chicago World's Fair. Emmanuel Louis Masqueray designed many of the Beaux Arts "palaces" for the exhibitions, which inhabited fifteen hundred buildings along seventy-five miles of roads. Mr. Ferris's gigantic Wheel was resurrected from storage in Chicago where it was first exhibited and shipped to St. Louis on 175 railroad cars. Built to rival the Eiffel Tower, the steel wheel was 265 feet tall with thirty-six school-bus sized "cars." The forty-eight-foot central axle was the largest single piece of iron ever forged. Capacity: over twenty-one hundred people. A ride cost fifty cents, but anyone could rent a car and have a party for their friends. One couple, riding ponies, got married in a Ferris Wheel car.

Nineteen and a half million people told their friends to "meet me in St. Louis," where Dr. Pepper and Puffed Wheat debuted. "Ferry floss," later known as cotton candy, was a big hit and, on one of the hottest days that summer the ice-cream cone was simultaneously invented by three vendors. After visiting the grand exhibition halls, most people hung out on The Pike, the fair's off-Broadway venue where performers of color, denied permission to perform in "The Main Picture" hall, were relegated. Scott Joplin, who composed "Cascades" to commemorate the fair's magnificent waterfall in front of Festival Hall, performed on The Pike. Anyone could be seen "coming down The Pike," where America's mixing bowl fermented. "Anthropological" exhibitions, amounting to human zoos, were a big feature. Families of Filipinos lived on site in thatched huts for months, freezing and undernourished. Chief Geronimo, officially a prisoner of war, was "on display" next to other Native American tribesmen—Eskimos, South American Indians, and African men, women, and children.

But by far the most visited attraction was "Beautiful Jim Key," the "educated horse." Jim was a phenom, a rock star; more than a sideshow, he *was* The Show. Not only could he count, perform basic arithmetic, and spell, he had an uncanny prescience that amazed and baffled anyone who saw him. The beautiful Alice Roosevelt, representing her father and accompanied by her future husband Nicholas Longworth, was present on Opening Day, the guest of honor at the Silver Horseshoe Building where "The Most Wonderful Horse in the World" dazzled all. Jim's loyal friend and trainer, Dr. William Key, a self-taught veterinarian and former slave from Shelbyville, Tennessee, was by his side.

Standing sixteen hands, Jim was a mahogany bay with a tail to die for, a star under his forelock, and one and a half socks on his far rear and near forefoot. An Arabian-Hambletonian cross, Jim was the offspring of the famous Arabian mare, Lauretta, reputedly stolen from Sheik Ahemid by a rascal Englishman who later sold her to an American circus, and Tennessee Volunteer, great-grandson of Rysdyk's Hamble-tonian (out of the Charles Kent Mare—a Norfolk Trotter—and by Abdullah, grandson of Messenger from the Darley Arabian line). Jim was an ugly duckling who parlayed his foal-hood disabilities—he didn't walk for weeks—into a bedroom inside Dr. Key's house (the horse was housebroken!) until he was moved to the barn as a yearling, where Dr. Key slept by his side for the rest their lives together.[7] Dr. Key was a whisperer; Jim was educated with kindness and their promoter Albert Rogers was a brilliant marketer. Don't forget that there were very few cars in the United States in 1905 and around twenty-two million horses. (There are around three million in the United States today.) Streets were not paved; horses were everywhere: pulling, pushing, plowing, hauling, halting, exhaling, defecating, and dying in the streets. Horses sounded the iambic tetrameter of daily life. Jim, Doc Key, and Albert launched the world's first successful movement promoting the humane treatment of animals in America.

Jim performed a little spelling test for Alice Roosevelt that day and, egged on by the crowd, he also spelled her sweetheart's name, tacking it on to her own, thereby predicting her marriage to Congressman Longworth from Ohio three years later. To great applause Jim the ham performed the Teddy Roosevelt grin. Jim liked to look out over the crowd, to take note of his admirers. Did Jim perchance see Smith or Higginson there?

The St. Louis fair, commemorating the Louisiana Purchase—the effective founding of the American Frontier—took place shortly after the Frontier was officially closed in 1890. Frederick Jackson Turner's "Frontier Thesis," which he had delivered at an architects' convention coinciding with the Chicago World's Fair, still held sway over Americans' psychic, and President Theodore Roosevelt embodied it. When John Singer Sergeant painted Roosevelt's official portrait for the White House in 1903 he is said to have captured two of the twenty-sixth president's "most salient characteristics, physical vitality and a self-assurance bordering on arrogance."[8]

Could it be that our Match, our contest of men on horseback and their foxhounds in the Virginia countryside, was also an exposition, an illustration of the central conflict in the regeneration myth: spontaneity versus authority, release versus control?

━◆━

But where lies the soul of fin de siècle? Who can say why, when, or from where an artist or even a scientist draws inspiration? Themes running through Western literature and philosophy in 1905 were, as at other times, rebelling against past excesses, in this case those of capitalism, materialism, and the way of life the Second Industrial Revolution had brought to most men and women in Europe and America. Advancements in science had brought great wealth and an explosion in the middle class, but with them came a longer and longer work week, bigger and bigger cities, faster and faster life. Oliver Wendell Holmes Jr. told Harvard's graduating class in his "The Soldier's Faith" speech on Memorial Day, 1895, "I once heard a man say, 'Where Vanderbilt sits, there is the head of the table. I teach my son to be rich.'" Lamenting the lessons his generation had learned in the Civil War, he went on to say, "war is out of fashion. Commerce is the great power." A half-century earlier Walt Whitman had called his countrymen to see, through his poetry, America's burgeoning landscape:

"immigrants continually coming / and landing; . . . old and new cities, solid, vast, / inland with paved streets . . . ceaseless vehicles, and commerce; / . . . the populace, millions upon millions . . . / the many-cylinder'd printing-press . . . / the electric telegraph . . . / the strong and quick locomotive, as it departs, panting, blowing / the steam-whistle; . . . [9] By 1905 all that and more had come to pass.

1905 was Albert Einstein's Miracle Year. He was the "discoverer of the quantum of light, the photon, founder of the quantum theory of solids, who at once realized that classical physics had reached its limits, a situation with which he never could make peace."[10] With the optimism of discovery comes the realization of everlasting change, for better or worse.

Like most of us, Einstein excelled in those subjects he loved, and neglected those he did not. He was a quiet nerdy kid who hated gymnastics, preferred to be alone, and also preferred to guide his own studies. He loathed arbitrary authority. His instructor at the Swiss Federal Polytechnic Institute in Zurich, Heinrich Friedrich Weber, once told young Albert, "You are a smart boy, Einstein, a very smart boy . . . but you have one great fault: you do not let yourself be told anything,"[11] It could be one of the world's most fortuitous mistakes that professor Weber refused to recommend Einstein for a postgraduate teaching position. So Einstein moved to Bern in 1902 on a tip that there may soon be an opening at the Swiss Federal Patent Office. There, without the responsibilities of teaching, Einstein enjoyed time enough for his own "thought experiments." It was in 1905 that, on a bus ride through Bern on his way to work, the Special Theory of Relativity came to him in a flash.[12] He said, "a storm opened in my mind."

"No one before or since has widened the horizons of physics in so short a time as Einstein did in 1905."[13] That March, a month before being awarded his PhD in Physics from the ETH in Zurich, Einstein completed the paper that was to earn him the 1921 Nobel Prize in Physics. Between March and December 1905 he wrote six papers; four were published in the prestigious journal *Annalen der Physik*, including that which contained the beautiful, deceptively simple, elegant little equation $E=mc^2$. Einstein's work that year, though he himself at the time did not fully realize its implications, would forever change our perception of reality.

His colleagues began comparing Einstein's 1905 to Isaac Newton's own *annus mirabilis*, 1666 (the year the apple dropped on his head), when during a break in classes due to a black-plague scare at Cambridge, Newton devised his theories on optics, calculus, and the Law of Gravitation. Abraham Pais described Einstein: "rarely lonely, mostly alone . . . easily accessible yet so apart, ever so friendly yet so distant."[14]

Would Smith or Higginson have heard about Einstein's Miracle Year? Possibly, but more probably neither would have understood it. As late as 1920, Relativity was "universally regarded as so profound that only twelve men in the entire world were believed able to fathom its depths."[15] What is certain is that after Einstein, everything, including space and time, was relative. Einstein's studies in the history and philosophy of science helped him to confront authoritative texts, to challenge "*a priori* givens," to question even Newton's Laws, for which he later wrote, "Newton, forgive me."[16]

While science seemed to provide all the answers, there emerged a longing for lost imagination, intuition, and fantasy. "Science," Oliver Wendell Holmes Jr. declared, "has pursued analysis until at last this thrilling world of colors and passions and sounds has seemed fatally to resolve itself into . . . the pale irony of the void." Philosophers—thinkers—in 1905 "walked a thin line between the excesses of positivism and irrational intuition. Anti-intellectualism took hold."[17] Meanwhile, a new medical condition arose, diagnosed by George Miller Beard: neurasthenia, or a lack of nerve—a paralysis of will. If Harry Worcester Smith accused Higginson of suffering from it, Higginson replied that Smith suffered from the opposite malady, whatever that was. Many Americans felt compelled to choose, on the basis of conflicting philosophies-cum-maladies, between the Old World and the New.

William James was the preeminent American philosopher of the time. A Harvard man, James founded the quintessentially American philosophical school of Pragmatism, which he intended to bridge the abyss between the "tough-minded pessimistic empiricists" and the "tender-minded dogmatic rationalists."[18] He did not see his pragmatism as a "truth," but as a problem-solving technique in search of consequence: "There can be no difference anywhere that doesn't make a difference elsewhere . . . a concrete fact . . . imposed on somebody, somehow, somewhere, and somewhen."[19] These days we see James's American pragmatism on bumper-stickers: *"Get er' done."* We are a nation of pragmatists.[20]

When James traveled to Edinburgh to deliver his lectures on religion and philosophy as the Gifford Lecturer on Natural Religion in 1901 and 1902, he admitted to the audience the novelty and perhaps audacity of an American come to lecture the Europeans. "It seems the natural thing for us to listen whilst the Europeans talk," he writes in Lecture I, "Religion and Neurology." "The contrary habit of talking whilst the Europeans listen, we have not yet acquired, and in him who first makes the adventure it begets a certain sense of apology being due for so presumptuous an act."[21] Henry Adams, James's friend, writes in *The Education of Henry Adams* (1886) that "for the first time in history, the American felt himself *almost* as strong as the Englishman. . . . He had thirty years to wait before he could feel himself stronger."

"Americans are eminently prophets," another friend of James's and fellow philosopher, Spanish-American George Santayana, writes: "They apply morals to public affairs; they are impatient and enthusiastic . . . they are men with principles, and fond of stating them . . . to exercise private judgment is not only a habit with them but a conscious duty. . . . America is full of vigor, goodness, and hope, such as no nation ever possessed before . . . a fearless people, and free from malice."[22] Santayana called America "an old head on young shoulders," exemplified by Mark Twain and Charles Ives—"steeped in unmitigated vernacular song and speech."[23]

Harry Worcester Smith was a card-carrying pragmatist who attended a polytechnic institute and studied mechanical engineering from experts at home and abroad. William James claimed that a polytechnic graduate is destined to "remain a cad, and not a gentleman, intellectually pinned down to his narrow subject, literal, unable to suppose anything different from what he has seen, without imagination atmosphere or mental perspective."[24] Smith had two favorite hunt horses: "Success" and "The Cad." If Smith heard or read Santayana's assessment of his countrymen, he probably extended the opinion to his American foxhound: self-reliant, full of vigor, fearless indeed.

Alexander Henry Higginson, on the other hand, graduated from Harvard and moved to the country to raise hounds and foxhunt. Higginson would have agreed more with William James's younger brother Henry, the consummate expat, an Anglophile almost from the day he was born. Henry James loved the very Englishness of England—even the weather! He called London "the capital of the human race."[25] His life's work compared and contrasted the European with the American ethos: "I aspire to write in such a way that it would be impossible to an outsider to say whether I am an American writing about England or an Englishman writing about America."[26] He writes about Americans' "argumentative national self-consciousness"—the chip on our collective shoulder; many thought him a snob.[27] Like Alexander Henry Higginson, Henry James exiled himself to England later in life, acquired British citizenship (though Higginson never did), and died there. Higginson would probably have agreed with James's assessment of his fellow Americans who "scatter themselves over Europe, by no means flattering to the national vanity—they are ill-made, ill-mannered, ill-dressed?" Higginson admired the upright, the patient and polite, those willing to queue up, the purely bred—even in a hound dog.

Such was the Spirit of the Times, the Zeitgeist, the Fin de Siècle, the Belle Époque, the Miracle Year. To some, decadence seemed to be at the root of the cultural pendulum, calling for a rebellion. To others it was a miraculous moment when anything seemed possible. Where did Smith and Higginson fit? Smith was the pragmatist; Higginson the traditionalist. Higginson was the happy conformist; Smith liked a good thought experiment. Smith and his hounds were mongrels—bold, forward, and independent to a fault. Higginson and his hounds were the refined, reserved elite—passively aggressive, methodical, accustomed to queuing, happy in a crowd of equals.

The men who fought The Match, though their hounds represented England and America, could only have been Americans—the only ones with anything to prove. If asked to match his English hounds against a pack of American hounds, an Englishman would have (politely, behind closed parlor doors, among fellow Englishmen) laughed in the American's face. Only two Americans—one who wanted to prove that we belonged among the best of the Old World, one who wanted to prove that we didn't—would have undertaken The Match. To Harry Worcester Smith only one kind of hound was fit for an American sportsman: a hound that emulated his countrymen—bold, self-assured, independent, heuristic, and quite possibly downright arrogant. To Higginson there was "no such thing as an American hound." England wasn't just the capital of civilized man, it was the home of the one and only foxhound.

4

Day One

Wednesday, November 1, 1905
Middlesex Hunt's First

"Mr. Higginson, having accepted the first day's trial for his Middlesex hounds, announced the meet for this morning at Welbourne and the time as 6:45."
—ALLEN POTTS, *RICHMOND TIMES-DISPATCH*, THURSDAY, NOVEMBER 2, 1905

"HE'S FIFTEEN MINUTES LATE," HARRY WORCESTER SMITH SAID TO Westmoreland "Morley" Davis. Harry was astride "The Cad," his champion steeplechaser on which he had won the $10,000 Steeplechase of America at Morris Park in 1900; Morley Davis was on his hunter "P.D.Q." Smith and Davis were among nearly one hundred mounted followers, as well as an equal number of folks intending to follow as best they could in buggies along local roads and byways. They were crowded onto the front lawn of Welbourne, a Georgian mansion, home of Colonel Richard Henry Dulany, a few miles as the crow flies north of Upperville. Everyone had hacked at least five miles to the meet. Dawn had been a half-hour hence. No dew. Not a drop of moisture. A stiff dry breeze lifted the horses' forelocks and manes. An alchemy of scent stirred, mixing, rising faintly, of predator and prey, of hunted and hunter: prey carrying predator chasing predator, now prey.

"Harry," Morley Davis said, "you must learn patience." Davis had recently bought a large farm, "Morvan Park," just outside Leesburg, intending to take up the agricultural trade, and had helped to establish the Loudoun Hunt Club in 1900. He was also destined to become Virginia's forty-eighth governor in the coming decade.

"Patience is for the faint-hearted," Smith said. His horse swiveled its hindquarters, bumping a lady's hunter next to him. Smith had taken a nasty fall back in '01, puncturing one lung, which had the nasty habit of hemorrhaging every now and then. Perhaps that was why he sat his horse so awkwardly hunched forward. "Pardon me, ma'am," he said, tipping his velvet hunt hat to the woman whose horse his had bumped. The woman, Mrs. Tom Pierce from Boston, was riding aside in an elegant black habit on her huge lady's hunter named "Nassaquag." A good friend of Mr. Higginson's, Mrs. Pierce moved off without acknowledging Mr. Smith of Lordvale.

"Tension is gaining ground," Colonel Dulany hollered from his front steps. The old gentleman stood, hands in his pockets, white-bearded chin jutting forward, feet spread shoulder-width apart as though he were surveying his troops again. His greatcoat fell open; his right arm hung at an awkward angle, the result of a war wound. He watched as the tops of the oaks, still holding their leaves as oaks are inclined to do, shook mightily with each gust. "This is more like a September wind," he commented to his guests, who moved about the broad two-story veranda between each of six columns. They had come for the spectacle, watching as riders circle their horses restlessly, waiting for Master Higginson to arrive.

There was a quality to the light on the colonel's lawn that morning, November 1, 1905, that reflected the atmosphere of excitement among the spectators and riders alike. Each horse had been washed and rubbed and brushed until it shone. The dark bays were polished mahogany, the chestnuts were copper pennies, the grays were dappled clouds, the blacks resembled glossy nuggets of coal. The eight or ten mounted women were riding aside, their hair pinned to perfection, their jackets brushed clean, one shiny stirruped boot peeking from beneath each spotless apron. The men of the Grafton persuasion wore grey coats with black collars and silver buttons, cream-colored britches, and black patent leather boots. Those from Middlesex wore scarlet coats with split tails overlapping their saddles, cream britches, and black dress boots. Some of the men were bare-headed, but some wore velvet hunting caps. Other riders wore their particular hunt's colors—light blue, dark green, or yellow for instance—on the collars of their dark blue or black coats. Twenty-six hunts from around the United States and Canada were represented on the colonel's front lawn.

"It's a marvelous site," one of the colonel's spectators said to no one in particular, and many nodded.

"Did you read where the *London Daily Mail* and the *New York Herald* will be reporting on this Match?" another asked.

"That's Allen Potts, over there," his friend replied, pointing. "He's the *Times-Dispatch* reporter from Richmond and some kind of official in this thing."

"It's really kind of a big deal," a woman standing next to him said.

"Yep, I suppose it is," the man said, sipping his port.

"You're damn right it is," the colonel said.

Smith shifted in his saddle, The Cad pawed. "Higginson's not even following today," Smith said. "He should have just let Cotesworth go on and do his job."

"Perhaps he will follow by road," Morley Davis said. Mrs. Davis was next to him. "What do you think, Marguerite?"

"I think he's late on purpose," she said.

"Maybe he's on to you, Mr. Smith," Ham Jackson, Smith's groom and whipper-in, said from the back of his pony, which stood like a statue next to the porch. Smith gave a grunt. His gift of the first day's hunt to Mr. Higginson had been based on the weather forecast—dry and windy—which should result in a blank day without so much as a single run. By his calculations, Smith reasoned that Day Two should carry more moisture, and he intended to be out as early as possible, down near Goose Creek where he knew a dog fox lived in an old log pile.

"I count ninety-eight riders, not including the Master," Ham Jackson said.

Bob Cotesworth, Higginson's hired professional huntsman, was on a tall bay hunter named "Nugent" in the center of the lawn—the image of a calm, knowledgeable, and skilled English hunt servant. He was raised in the English Midlands and there he trained at the best kennels including the Belvoir and Brocklesby, had served as huntsman for the Earl of Bathurst, immigrated to America when Foxhall Keene formed his drag pack at Meadow Brook on Long Island, and gone over to Higginson when Keene had dissolved that pack in 1903. America was a fine place, but it wasn't England and in his opinion these Americans had a lot to learn about proper foxhunting. He looked like a grizzled little old man on the ground; in the saddle he was a prince. His backbone stacked itself in perfect alignment over his horse's spine, his feet hanging properly beneath his hips, not a tense muscle, just infinite calm and strength. Thirty-seven Middlesex hounds, eighteen and a half couple, shifted in a tight bunch around his horse's legs like a flock of blackbirds in the treetops. Every now and then Cotesworth clucked or grumbled something to the pack or an individual hound. "Visitor," he said, in a low almost growl. "Here, here, laddie." Visitor looked up. He was Cotesworth's favorite, a fine upstanding hound. All the hounds watched Cotesworth as if he were their God and, as a matter of fact, he was. Only he, Bob Cotesworth, could hunt them as they should be hunted. He might not be the Master, but he was the best English huntsman America had. With his help, Master Higginson had chosen the best English hounds and brought them to America. Cotesworth's pride showed in the stonework of his features. He didn't give a damn how late the Master was; he and his hounds could sit there all day if need be. Let those bastards in grey stew a bit, was his idea. His hounds would wait, as they were trained, until, and not before, their huntsman asked them to move. One hound strayed to a bush to piss and Bob's son, Ed, who was his hired whipper-in, cracked his whip yelling "ooy." The hound trotted back to her pack and sat obediently.

"They're a beautiful pack, you have to admit, Harry," Morley Davis said. "Mostly bitches out today."

"If you like Shorthorns," Smith said. "Cows that is."

"They are awfully heavy," Mrs. Davis said. Her horse nodded as if in agreement and she rubbed his neck.

"They're pigeon-toed and knock-kneed," Smith said. "They look like they've been bred to box as heavy-weights."

"I don't know how he tells them apart, they look exactly alike, down to the tips of their tails," Morley said.

A servant in the colonel's livery came by carrying a silver tray holding a dozen silver glasses of the colonel's port.

The Cad shied and snorted at the shiny silver thing. Smith said "No thanks," but Morley said, "Don't mind if I do."

"Twenty minutes late," Smith reminded everyone.

As the sun rose above the Bull Run Mountains, the Loudoun Valley remaining in their shadow, their parent range in the west, the Blue Ridge, took on a golden glow as their natural blue haze dispersed in the wind. Since most of the leaves had fallen, the rocky ridges showed white against a sky streaked with high thin mares' tails that changed color with each passing moment. A red-tailed hawk shrieked overhead as the mice most likely dove for cover in the colonel's thick pastures.

Waiting. Waiting. Shifting, jostling, snorting, pawing horses eager to be off. Nervous, excited, anxious humans steering them through the crowd in a continuous effort to maintain calm. Each breath, human or equine, mixed with the morning air, sending yet another molecule of odor into the atmosphere for the hounds to catch and assimilate into their knowledge of the earth's rich pallet of scent. At 7:45 a.m., one half-hour after the agreed-upon time, all heads, human and equine, raised at the coming clatter of hoofs and buggy wheels on the road to Welbourne. Alexander Henry Higginson's groom steered the runabout onto the circular drive and proceeded parade-like, as riders nudged their horses out of the way, to the front steps where the colonel stood.

"Good morning, Mr. Higginson," the colonel said. "Better late than never. All are assembled for your first day of hunting, as you can see."

Higginson climbed down and walked a bit stiffly to Cotesworth, the hounds sniffing his hands and boots, eager for the Master's praise. One was so bold as to jump and place his paws on Higginson's shoulders, but he was quickly reprimanded with a grunt from Cotesworth. A brief quiet conference between Master and servant was followed by Higginson turning to the crowd and announcing, "May I have your attention please?"

"Here we go," Smith said. "He's probably going to call the whole thing off."

"I wish a very good morning to each of you," Higginson called to the crowd, tipping his hat to the colonel. "Mr. Cotesworth is ready to set off for the first cover at Beaverdam Creek a few miles from here. Mrs. Pierce has the field today," he said, pointing to the woman Harry's horse had bumped. "Please pay close attention to her wishes, and please be sure to protect the valuable land over which we will run today. Report any damages done to fences or property when the day is done and I will reimburse the landowner forthwith. Mr. Cotesworth will draw at least three coverts, but as the scent isn't likely to be very good today due to this wind, he will withdraw within two hours' time if the hounds have not found. I will follow in my runabout today. There will be plenty of hill-toppers watching from afar. Have a wonderful time, everyone!"[1]

"The fun begins," Smith said to Morley, kicking The Cad into a trot to stay in front of the crowd. "Keep up, or be left," he said over his shoulder. "Ham, meet me back here," he called to Ham Jackson, who intended to escort the colonel across the countryside to watch the show from a distance. No one knew better where to be and how to get there than Ham Jackson. The colonel watched as the crowd of riders jockeyed for position heading down the road. Mr. and Mrs. Davis were in the middle, Harry Worcester Smith was up front next to Mrs. Pierce, and a group of young ladies on their big hunters was near the back. One of the young ladies, his granddaughter Eva "Terry" Dulany on her beautiful bay named "Welbourne Bachelor," waved to the colonel.

They trotted east down Welbourne Road and turned left into a fifty-acre field of winter wheat where they picked up a canter to catch up to Mrs. Pierce. Cotesworth and the hounds had already cleared a stone wall at the opposite end of the field. As she approached the three-foot wall, partially crumbled but jumpable, Mrs. Pierce nudged Nassaquag and he skipped over it like it was a fallen branch. The rest of the field spread out to find their own line and followed, one by one or two by two. The first and last jumps of the day are always the hardest, when the horses are still fresh and liable to take a misstep or tired and more likely to hook a foot and trip. When Mr. Paul Whitin, a friend of Smith's from Whitin, Massachusetts, asked his hunter to jump the wall, it took off too soon and he went off over his horse's left shoulder. The good horse stood still until Whitin, whose pride was badly damaged, but nothing else, could climb back on.

A hundred yards or so on the far side of the wall, the field came to a dense thicket of shrub near the mouth of Beaverdam Creek, where

Cotesworth had sent the hounds on their first draw. Up until the very moment when Cotesworth waved them into the thicket with a flick of his wrist, the hounds remained in a tight bunch around his horse. The whips galloped around to the east and west of the thicket—an acre or so of low-growing briars and brambles—in order to cut off any hounds that may dash out in the wrong direction if a run commenced.

"Cover hoick, cover hoick," Cotesworth called to his hounds. "Eloo-in, eloo-in, eloo-in," he repeated, encouraging them to spread throughout the thicket and search for scent.

"Terrible scent today, I would imagine," someone said.

"Too windy," another said.

"It sounds as though he is speaking a foreign language to those hounds," a woman said.

"He is, practically," a man said. "Can't understand a word, but I suppose the hounds can."

"Of course they can," Mrs. Pierce said. "Now will everyone please be quiet!"

Harry Worcester Smith stood The Cad next to Mrs. Pierce's horse, though she ignored him. He didn't speak either. He wanted to watch Cotesworth's hound work. He'd hunted many times behind packs of English hounds both on drag hunts with fake scent, and on live hunts after real foxes, but he'd never hunted behind the Middlesex hounds or Cotesworth. They were impressive in their own way, very organized, very systematic, like a well-oiled loom. They stuck together as if they were tethered to one another by invisible threads several yards long. Occasionally one hound in particular would let her tongue fly, but Smith was fairly certain that she was just a babbler, unable to keep quiet even though she had nothing to tell, like some women he knew. He also knew for a fact that there was no fox in this particular patch of scrub. There used to be an old dog fox who kenneled here during the daylight hours, but he had moved out months ago, according to the colonel. Smith had suggested a different coppice, but Cotesworth must have decided on this one as soon as he'd seen it. It did look like a likely spot, and there could very well be a hint of scent a day or so old left from a fox's footpads, but in his opinion these English hounds didn't have a chance in hell of catching it.

Smith watched as what was clearly the lead hound circled and looped within the scrub, searching, searching. The northeast wind was in the riders' faces carrying a faint whiff of wild sage as the hounds stirred the ground beneath their feet. The sun was too high, the wind was too strong, all signs pointed toward a blank day—at least that's what Smith hoped for.

"Edawick, Edawick," Cotesworth chanted to the hounds. "Yoi, rouse him, Visitor. Rouse him, my boys." Though their sterns waved like tall grass in the wind, not one hound's tongue wagged. After about fifteen minutes Cotesworth lifted their heads with a blast from his huntsman's horn and called them to him, intending to head to another covert to try again. Within seconds the pack was with him, not a straggler in sight, and he took off north by northeast along the creek. Dense riparian scrub and young-growth trees lined the creek, but the fields were open and mown and the footing was excellent. He came to a roadway, where he scrambled across a couple of hedges on either side and made away into the next field, soon out of sight. Mr. Higginson in his runabout and several other interested followers stood along the roadway watching the hunters jump.

Mrs. Pierce found a set of stone walls on either side of the road and her handy hunter jumped them both cleanly to follow on. Smith was close on her horse's heels, perhaps too close, for she glanced back at him in hopes that he would back off, but Smith had no intention of letting Cotesworth get too far out of sight. Mr. Chamberlain, a friend of Higginson, on his horse "Warbonnet," followed them both handily, as did the rest of the field. They had a fine gallop across another well-kept field and soon came upon Cotesworth working his hounds in a coppice of young pine, the place Smith had suggested at the meeting. As each rider caught up to the rest of the field they pulled their horses up to stand or pace, breathing and snorting from the brief gallop. Everyone was eager for a real run, a fox gone away to the other side of the county, the world for that matter. Everyone was eager for a chase.

Again Cotesworth hollered his strange hound language. Again nothing, no fox in the pines, no foxes thereabouts. Smith watched, thinking that he would have let his hounds stick around longer in the last cover, let them range left and right much farther than the English hounds had been allowed. He knew that his American hounds had good cold noses, far better at finding old "cold" scent than these English hounds who were bred to hunt the moist floodplains of the English Midlands. He was eager to show Higginson and Cotesworth how it was done in Virginia. He felt practically imprisoned by the tight control Cotesworth held over his pack. There were nearly forty hounds, all very fit, all well trained, but where was their freedom to work? Where was their initiative? Smith felt like he was watching a crowd of Brits queue for the loo.

Again Cotesworth lifted his hounds with a blast from his horn to take them off to another covert. Again the riders followed across fields separated by farm lanes and larger roads. Though there hadn't yet been a run, the riders were having plenty of fun jumping. At one sticky spot Chamberlain on Warbonnet jumped a rail fence about four feet high, only to be confronted by a blind ditch into which the horse stumbled on the other side, sending Chamberlain in his beautiful pink coat into the mud where he rolled a couple of times and sat up cussing. Warbonnet was caught by another Middlesex member and brought back on a loose rein. Chamberlain, with his filthy backside, climbed back aboard.

After three blank coverts Cotesworth got the signal from Higginson to call it a day, but just then a country farmer in old overalls stopped in the road to say that he knew where a dog fox kenneled every day, "Not too far from here." Higginson told Cotesworth to give it a go. The covert was deeper in the woods. Maybe, with a break from the wind in a quiet damp spot where the scent could hang, they could stir the old fox out. It was almost ten o'clock and they hadn't yet had even one short run.

The field approached another road and spread out to find spots to jump yet another stone wall. Smith found a good spot where the walls on both sides of the road were well laid, jumped them both with two strides between and galloped off behind Mrs. Pierce. Terry Dulany, the colonel's granddaughter, urged Bachelor to follow where she believed they had jumped and cleared the first wall nicely, only to find a wire fence looming at least four feet high on the other side of the road. Allen Potts pulled up to watch as the young woman, realizing the fix she was in and unable to stop in time, dug her spur into Bachelor's near side, whacked him with her whip on his far side, gave him his head and sailed over the dangerous wire in fine form. Potts gave a hoot of appreciation as she galloped away. His copy for the next morning's *Times-Dispatch* would definitely include *that* fine little piece of riding.

The farmer was dead wrong about the dog fox in the wood. At 10:30 a.m. after yet another blank covert, Cotesworth called his hounds to home and turned back toward Middleburg. They were at least twelve miles from the colonel's home where breakfast would be waiting, but the huntsman was obliged to take the hounds back to their home away from home. He was disappointed that his hounds had not found. He had hoped to show some good sport, some good English sport. Alas, it was not in the wind today. But his hounds had performed well, under the circumstances. They were not used to this country. It was different from Massachusetts and so completely different from England that he felt the disadvantage as a sort of pain in his heart. He wanted so to prove his hounds.

"I say the day was a blank," Dr. McEachran said to Higginson. They were on the veranda at Oakley looking south at a stunning view of the Piedmont. "Too dry. No scent whatsoever."

"How can you say the day was blank?" Jim Maddux, who was standing nearby, said. "Just because the run was blank doesn't mean the day was blank. After all, the hounds started a full forty-five minutes after the designated time and an hour and a half after daybreak. Seems to me there could have been a fox started somewhere in that critical time and my report to the scribe will say as much."

"Then we shall disagree," McEachran said.

"We can agree that no fox was started," Hal Movius said. "That much is certain."

5

"Keep On Going"

Harry Worcester Smith (1865–1945)

BORN BETWEEN AMERICA'S NINETEENTH- AND TWENTIETH-CENTURY'S
wars, Harry Worcester Smith's dates resonate harshly with we who
live in the twenty-first century. Where those wars seemed resolute
and honorable, so right from wrong (from either side), fightable, even
winnable—not for just *a* cause, but *the* cause against *the* Enemy—our
wars seem endless. Harry not only fit the mold—good conscientious
citizen—he *made* the mold: industrial "harmonizer" (his word), erudite
sportsman, bibliophile, art connoisseur and collector, peerless amateur,
self-promoter, opinionated capitalist, hard-headed egotist. He built his
first career on his and his wife's ancestors' legacies and a second in what
we call industrial consulting or mergers and acquisitions—conglomerate building—which he named "harmonizing." He was an industrialist
when America was industrial and industrious, riding the crest of the
second revolution by that name. He made and won several fortunes in
cotton weaving and horses. He liked to say that "it is all right to have
one's fun, but it is poor policy not to earn the wherewithal to keep said
fun going." He could be accused of squandering his wherewithal on the
quintessential rich-man's sport—foxhunting—but to Harry foxhunting,
steeplechasing, racing thoroughbred horses and hounds weren't just pas-
times; they were the key to America's successes at home and abroad.
Sportsmen, and a few women, knew the value of a healthy body, a mind
broadened by wide-open vistas, the psychology of unhindered movement, and the concept of conquering a respected enemy. Harry Worcester Smith liked to say that he did everything, always and forever "For the
Sake of Sport in America."

He was a second-generation American of English descent, a Smith from Smithville, a hamlet of mills in central Massachusetts near Barre on the Ware River, where his grandfather, John, and John's brothers had settled at the turn of the nineteenth century. It seems the water of the Ware River "has a chemical quality especially adapting it to cleansing wool of its impurities. . . . . Here the grandfather of Harry Worcester Smith made a fortune with cotton cloth and American labor."[1] John Smith is known in Barre for saving the village's majestic pine trees, which the town's selectmen had threatened to chop down for fear that someone may crash into one while driving at night. John saved them by promising to whitewash the offending trees and keep them painted "fifteen feet above the ground." Harry's father, Charles Worcester Smith, born in nearby West Boylston in 1823, carried on his father's community stewardship by planting an avenue of Maples in Smithville and continuing his weaving business there.

Harry's mother, Josephine Caroline Lord, was born on land in Lyme, Connecticut, given to her family by the Mohegan sachem Uncas. "When I was one-year old," she writes in *A Sketch of Mrs. C. W. Smith's Life Written by Herself, 1909*, "my father took the family west" by steamboat, canal boat, and Prairie Schooner to Canton, Illinois, where he bought a thousand acres of virgin prairie for $1 an acre, "the most fertile farming land, beautiful and rich with hills and meadows and streams."[2] Their first house was a two-room cabin where Josephine slept in a loft with carpets on the ceiling "to keep the wind and snow from blowing in." Her family raised pigs and cattle and "a great many horses." The family's farming methods would make a locavore glad: "Our pork was so much more healthful than the pork in the East, because of the fact that our hogs lived in the woods eating acorns and roots and such things, and were fed on corn and milk and buttermilk at night." She loved horses and, to protect their herd of cattle from wolves, she and her siblings "would ride way out onto the prairie, for there were no fences, and drive the cows home in the evening."

Charles Smith had traveled to Canton "for his health" in 1855, where he spotted Josephine sitting next to a wood stove at a church service on a cold day that winter. "She was small, she was plump, she had very black eyes, and very rosy cheeks," her friend Mary E. Kellogg writes in

Josephine's book. Charles left town without introducing himself to the pretty girl, but when he mentioned her to a fellow stagecoach passenger the man offered to pen an introduction and Charles got off at the next town to turn back and make her acquaintance. He stuck around so long to court Josephine that he had to wire home to Smithville for more money, and the Canton townies began calling him "the strapped Yankee."

The couple married in April 1856, and Charles took Josephine back east where he became partners with his brothers in their father's woolen mills. "Fearing that I might be homesick, he bought me a very beautiful cream-colored saddle horse and outfit, which afforded me great pleasure," Josephine writes. The horse, named "Cub," lived to be thirty-four years old, "the nursery horse" who taught her children how to ride and drive. It isn't hard to see where Harry found his horse sense.

In the 1860s Charles moved his family to Worcester. "The Smith's barn was the best barn in Worcester and held the best horses to be found in the town in those days," writes Robert Morris Washburn, who grew up next door to the Smith family at 39 Elm Street and later served in the Massachusetts House of Representatives and Senate.[3] "The first two outdoor interests of Mr. [Charles] Smith were his horses and his flowers," Washburn writes. "[Charles] stood for peace among the children of the neighborhood. Mrs. Smith was a landmark. She was tireless. She always forgot herself and always remembered her children and their friends. As a mother, she was a symbol of love."[4] Harry was one of six children—five boys and a girl. Born November 5, 1865, he was christened Henry Witter Smith after a family friend, once the superintendent of the Boston, Barre and Gardner Railroad, "which did not begin in Boston, go through Barre or stop at Gardner."[5] Sometime before 1900 he changed his name to Harry Worcester, his middle name reflecting his grandmother Clarissa Worcester Smith.

Every morning Charles drove his buggy five miles to his mill, a twenty-minute commute northeast of Worcester. "Back then . . . when it was a common sight to see cows driven through Elm Street to pasture on Newton Hill . . . everyone knew personally each horse in Worcester . . . men showed their skill, taste and money in the horses they bought and the townspeople came out to sit in judgment there upon."[6] Besides Cub in the Smith's barn, there was "a high-strung chestnut, the best road horse in Worcester County" and a "light-weight brown horse of splendid show action owned by Harry Worcester Smith."[7]

Between the Washburns and the Smiths, there were fourteen children—eleven boys and three girls. The neighborhood kids called Harry "Bits" or "Biddy." While the Washburns were a scholarly bunch, the Smiths were hooligans, only at times "becoming human beings and like other children." In the basement of the barn the Smiths kept a few pigs and on the second floor there lived an eagle, some caged pigeons, a family of rabbits, one or two goats, a pony, and a monkey. Harry, a hound man from the very beginning, also kept his prized greyhounds, "Friday Night," "Mother Demdike," and "Honor Bright," in the barn. Harry's brother Chetwood owned a pack of beagles.

A biographical sketch of Harry Worcester Smith, published by the United Press Syndicate in 1915, reads, as the Who's Who genre is apt to do, like a slightly embarrassing, decidedly cheesy, overblown resume from an eager collegiate, clearly an autobiography written in third person: "In considering the career of Harry W. Smith, one is impressed by the variety of really important things that he has found time to do."[8] He attended "the public schools in his native city," Worcester High School, before entering the Worcester County Free Institute of Industrial Science, later known as Worcester Polytechnic Institute (WPI). He must have been less than attentive to his studies, because the faculty minutes from January 17, 1885, note that, "having fallen below the average mark of 60," Smith and a classmate named Wilson, ceased "to be members of the Institution."

Could it have been his already blooming interest in hounds that distracted him from his algebra? Before flunking out he was implicated in at least one incident that went down in the annals of the school's best pranks. In the fall of 1884, which would have been Harry's first term, superintendent Milton Higgins's horse "Buckskin" went missing. "Buckskin must have been a very good-natured steed and one with an excellent sense of balance," writes H. F. Taylor in his history of the school, *Seventy Years of WPI*.[9] Several boys, no one was saying who, led the dorsal-striped dun up two flights of spiraling stairs into the tower of Boynton Hall, "to be picketed in the room where faculty and students gathered for morning devotions." It took a wing and a prayer to get him down again—a problem "too involved for mechanical engineers, so a veterinary was called." Blanketed, padded, and blindfolded with his legs tied together, old Buckskin was lowered "on skids with the aid of block and tackle . . . students cheering the proceedings were dispersed by a squad of police."

Harry claimed he had nothing to do with it. "As luck would have it I was in New York at the Madison Square Garden Dog Show at the time . . . consequently, I had a clear alibi."[10] He was showing his greyhounds at The Garden; two of his hounds, "Memnon" and "Friday Night" were American champions.[11] The WPI student body took a vow of silence to protect the guilty and it wasn't until some years later that they fessed up and Harry was indeed exonerated. But his reputation must not have excluded him from suspicion, "for 2 or 3 days, Smith of the junior Class stood out quiet prominent," Harry writes years later to Mr. A. D. Butterfield of the Alumni Committee.

"Desiring to complete his training along the lines that he had chosen," the United Press Syndicate's profile continues, "he later went abroad and took courses in the Chemnitz Technical School, Germany; the Glasgow School of Design in Scotland, and the Bradford Technical School of Bradford England." Well done Harry. But *why*? Why *Europe*? And *why then*?

Young Harry had begun hanging around the Crompton family home in pursuit of George Crompton's daughter Mildred. George was born in Lancashire, England, the son of William Crompton whose early patented fancy color loom had left George with a "golden heirloom."[12] William, who sailed to America in 1836, was once asked why he had left England. "I was afraid," he replied. "The workmen disliked me because I was constantly finding ways to cut down the amount of labor required to do certain jobs. I determined to emigrate to America, where there was less agitation against new ideas." Indeed, the father of a young man named Andrew Carnegie was an out-of-work weaver, displaced by the likes of William Crompton's time-saving looms. William's son George became the proprietor of the Crompton Loom Works, leading employer in Worcester in the 1880s and leading manufacturer of "closed shed" looms in the world at the time. His home was an enormous arched and gabled Elizabethan mansion designed by Eldridge Boyden and fashioned, according to his wife Mary's wishes, after "Holland House" in London. It was made of dark red stone, had one of those new-fangled "tennis" courts as well as croquet courts, and was surrounded by elaborate rose gardens that sloped down Providence Hill just east of town. "There was but one estate in Worcester which could be called an estate—Mariemont of the Cromptons on Providence Hill."[13]

"George Crompton called me into his library one day," Harry explains in a letter to Charles Baker, Secretary of the WPI Alumni Association. "[Crompton] asked me, 'Harry, what are you going to do about it?' I thought he meant his daughter, and said I did not know. He said he meant about my education, and went on and said that if I would place myself in his hands he would, after I got through the next examinations, take care of me."[14] The exams didn't go so well, but George Crompton was a man of his word. "Naturally," Harry continues, "when an offer like this came from Mr. Crompton I took it up, and I have never been sorry."

It must have been sometime in 1884 or 1885 that George Crompton called young Harry into his library. Harry would have been just about twenty years old; he was nineteen in 1883, the spring his father committed suicide. "Saturday's announcement that Charles Worcester Smith, one of Worcester's most widely known and successful business men, had committed suicide by cutting his throat with a razor, was shocking and sorrowful beyond expression," the *Worcester Spy* reported on May 5, the Monday after his death.[15] "Mr. Smith returned from a southern trip . . . taken for his health . . . which has not been of the best this winter, although his condition had not been such as to cause serious alarm among his friends," the paper reports. Lifelong health problems must have sent Harry's father abroad often, as it was on a trip "for his health," to Illinois that he had met Josephine, back in 1856. Charles was not only a woolen manufacturer; he was also president of the Mechanics National Bank and director of the Worcester and Nashua Railroad as well as a trustee of the Worcester County Institution for Savings. "Truthfulness, modesty and affection" were his singular attributes, according to the Reverend Rush R. Shippen of Washington, D.C., who spoke at Charles's funeral. It was presided over by a minister from the Church of the Unity and held at the Smith's house at the corner of Chestnut and Elm, where now stands the

Worcester Historical Museum. Josephine Caroline Smith and Charles Worcester Smith had been married twenty-seven years; Charles was fifty-four. Unhappily, Charles's father, John, had also committed suicide.[16] Josephine had long ago formulated her life's refrain: "keep on going."[17]

Years later, when asked by the *Worcester Evening Post*, "What was the best investment you ever made?" Harry set aside his industrial, and even his equine-related accomplishments, to remember time spent with his father. His father taught him the value of "trudging the hills and dales of Worcester County, learning the names of the trees and the calendar of the wild flowers . . . finding where the Arethusa grew and the beautiful Pitcher plant grew . . . learning to walk and ride out with health . . . the ability to recognize the wonders of the Universe."[18]

Lucky boy, Harry Worcester Smith, to find a man like George Crompton to step in as a father figure for the young industrialist. Crompton's Loom Works was in its prime in the late 1800s. George Crompton's name appeared on some two hundred patents, which added 60 percent to the production capacity of cotton weaving machinery, while saving 50 percent on labor.[19] Harry couldn't have picked a better mentor. It was George Crompton who must have encouraged Harry to take additional classes at the Lowell School of Design, associated with Massachusetts Institute of Technology at the time, and sent him overseas to study in Germany and Great Britain, the two great manufacturing centers of the first, and early in the second, Industrial Revolutions.

When George Crompton died, in1886, Harry set out on his own and bought the Wachusett Mill in Worcester with $50,000 from his father's estate. Worcester was a beautiful little inland city at the time. Charles Dickens visited Worcester and read at Mechanics' Hall on March 23, 1868, calling Worcester "a pretty New England town with clean white houses." Harry's new venture didn't turn out well; he lost his first fortune on it, but wound up with a pretty patent on a lucrative innovation in cotton weaving, the Standard Automatic Color Loom, which made color weaving possible in cotton and silk gingham.[20] By leasing this and other of his patents associated with cotton weaving, around forty altogether, to various weaving factories in New England, he made his second fortune, "and deposited in the bank one-half million dollars."[21] He and Mildred

Crompton were married on October 16, 1892, and Harry became a patent expert. He held that post at the Crompton and Knowles Loom Works, an industrial conglomerate, formed in 1897 by the merger of the Crompton Loom Works, manufacturer of "closed shed" looms, and their competitor, the Knowles Loom Works, manufacturer of "open shed" looms. He also made himself indispensable to other manufacturers who began to find themselves evermore mired in patent disputes as advances in industrial machinery progressed. "He consolidated the Crompton-Knowles Loom Works with the Crompton-Thayer Loom Works into the largest manufacturers of weaving machinery in the world," the United Syndicate Press release states, but the article is quick to point out that "he has always studiously avoided the methods of the promoter, but has worked hard to bring opposing interests together and has naturally profited by the crystallization of his plans." Along those lines, he took up Thomas G. Plant's case against the United Shoe Machinery Companies of Boston, which went to the US Supreme Court and won Harry a verdict of $350,000.

Considering that, in the nineteenth century, "the greatest statesmen, soldiers and jurists of England and America were ardent and earnest fox hunters," Harry Worcester Smith was once again in the right place at the right time[22]—not on the links or the courts, but in the hunt field. Businessmen spent their mornings in the hunt fields on Long Island, in Worcester County, Massachusetts, or Chester County, Pennsylvania, and their afternoons in their offices in New York, Boston, and Philadelphia. Harry took advantage of the national sporting trend, which was promulgated and proclaimed by the progressive politician and Smith's friend, Teddy Roosevelt. He met, shook hands with, probably slapped the back of, and no doubt schmoozed every budding sportsman he could find. By 1900 Harry and Mildred had two children and Harry moved his family to his mother's family's country estate, "Lordvale," named for her ancestor Thomas Durfree Lord, in nearby North Grafton. He bought the Kinnicutt house on Elm Street in Worcester, next door to the Smith family's barn, and moved it to Lordvale, making it into a twelve-room, three-story mansion valued at $100,000 in the 1920s. He started and "incubated" the Grafton Country Club, where the motto was "to each his pleasure," and the desire was to "bring within reach of [Worcester], wholesome

English outdoor life, riding, shooting and hunting.[23] Harry provided the horses; novice members provided their guts. He was a "central figure" of the prestigious Brookline Country Club originally established in 1882 as an equestrian and social club outside Boston. Soon his name became synonymous with "sportsman."

And then there were the horses; he and Mildred were both champion four-in-hand drivers based at Lordvale. Harry's high-stepping pacers "Sky-High" and "Sue Woodstock" won three National Horse Shows at Madison Square Garden against the Vanderbilts "with limited capital, with his brains, he beat them with their money."[24] He rescued "Ting-a-Ling" from the Worcester Street Car Company after the horse ran away with a car full of passengers and used the grey as his near-lead horse in his famous four-in-hand team.[25] Riding his mare "Sure-Pop," Harry beat Sidney Holloway, on Holloway's American champion "Chappie," in the high jump in 1896 at Boston's indoor Mechanics Hall: "when Smith, bare-headed with hair curling ... headed that mare for those bars, the whole gallery stood."[26] In his thirties, he took up steeplechasing. He won the Genesee Valley Point-to-Point—an old-fashioned steeplechase between two points kept secret until the very moment riders take off—four times. In his violet and white colors, he won the gentlemen's Whitney race at Saratoga in 1897 and the Meadowbrook Hunt Cup on Long Island for two years consecutively in 1898 and 1899. He won the Champion Steeplechase of America for $10,000 against six professional jockeys at Morris Park in 1900 on "The Cad," a horse he'd bought for $150. He won $8,000 on "Sacket," taking first at the Grand National Steeplechase at Sheepshead Bay in 1901, and the Hempstead and Calvert Cups the same year at Baltimore. Between 1898 and 1903, he was considered *the* gentleman rider in America.

Harry and Mildred had begun foxhunting with Major Austin Wadsworth's Genesee Valley hounds in the late 1890s. According to her brother, George, Mildred "was able to take the fences encountered in that sport."[27] At first Harry liked to hunt well enough, but he found that Major Wadsworth's English hounds didn't amount to much. "There was no more hospitable gentleman in all America than W. Austin Wadsworth," Smith writes in his unpublished autobiography, "but hospitality does not make a foxhunter nor an open sideboard a good fox cover. Unfortunately he did not jump, but led his horse over obstacles; this of course made it necessary for rails to be taken down so that, if hounds really ran, he was soon out of the picture . . . there was the pageant of the chase and that was all." The sport had not yet become Smith's passion.

Then, in 1893, Major Wadsworth invited Mr. Thomas Hitchcock, owner of a pack of hounds bred in Hickery, Tennessee, by James M. Avent, to hunt the Genesee Valley territory and Harry went along for the ride. That day Harry said that he saw a light shown on a pack of hounds that he thought he'd never see in America. He gave up steeplechasing and took up foxhunting. Mr. Hitchcock's "black and tan pack showed Mr. Smith that a pack of fox killing American hounds could really give great sport in the States and account for their quarry."[28]

From the Genesee Valley, Smith went to Virginia at the invitation of H. Rozier Dulany to hunt behind a pack of black and tan Virginia hounds owned by Rozier's cousin Richard Hunter Dulany and the latter's father, Colonel Richard Henry Dulany of Upperville. Initial impressions meant everything to Harry Worcester Smith; he took nothing lightly. He bet his reputation as a hound man, as a rider, and as a foxhunter on those Virginia hounds. In 1903 he bought the foundation for his first pack of American hounds: one stallion from Frank Bywaters, Virginia's leading commercial hound breeder, and two from Kentucky breeders, Steve Walker and Senator E. K. Renaker. He writes of training the Grafton hounds on family camping expeditions with Mildred and the children to Lake Manchaug near Sutton, south of Worcester: "The camp was made up of six or eight tents, for myself, the children, their friends, and the servants, and a night lunch cart which we converted into a caravan for Mrs. Smith. . . . There we were, horses, hounds, tents, food, swimming, canoeing, fishing and the best of fox-hunting within a stone's throw."[29]

The Kentucky hounds, "Simple" and "Sinner," would prove to be his best stallion hounds and invaluable to him in The Match. He began hunting Worcester County foxes with his new "Grafton Hounds" and, always pursuing recognition for his exploits, encouraged the local Brunswick Fur Club to hold the first foxhound show in America in 1903. From then on Harry was a venatical fanatic and his new motto was: "My line is the line of the foxes; my pace is the pace of the pack."

6

Day Two

Thursday, November 2, 1905
Grafton Hunt's First

"The ladies all went remarkably well."
—ALLEN POTTS, *RICHMOND TIMES-DISPATCH*, FRIDAY,
NOVEMBER 3, 1905

STARS WERE STILL OUT AND DAWN ONLY BARELY GRAZED THE HORIZON AS Harry Worcester Smith and his team set out from Oakley toward Leithton near the Pot House north of Middleburg for his first day as Master and huntsman in the Great Hound Match of 1905. Rozier Dulany, Colonel Dulany's favorite nephew, was Smith's host for The Match. Smith stabled the seven horses he'd brought by train with him from Massachusetts to Virginia at Oakley, plus fourteen hounds, thirteen of which—six and a half couple—he was committed to using in The Match. Two horses belonging to Allen Potts, three of Paul Whitin's, six belonging to the Westmoreland Davises, three of Smith's first whip Mal Richardson's, and two of Mr. James Roosevelt's were also stabled at Oakley.[1] The party of horses, hounds, and humans trooping off down the Ashby Gap Turnpike toward the same hunting ground that the Middlesex had tried the day before disturbed the morning's quiet with snorts, whines, and whinnies and possibly a yawn or two from the humans. Harry Worcester Smith, however, was wide awake.

Smith was primed. He'd already been in Upperville for well-nigh a month riding, walking, exploring the countryside alongside Rozier and Ham, with and without his hounds. The rules of the match, drawn up in

June, stipulated that "neither pack is to be hunted in the Piedmont Valley before November 1st," and technically Smith had not done so, but he had been "roading" his hounds—trotting them up and down the lanes and byways of Loudoun and Fauquier Counties—for two weeks. He'd been coming to hunt with the Dulanys since the late nineties; he knew the country well. In fact, with the help of Hal, Rozier, Hunter, and Colonel Dulany, he had drawn a map of the Piedmont hunt country superimposed on a US government survey map of the area. The map had been published in *Rider and Driver* in October, which meant that the Higginson crowd had had a chance to "see" the country. Still, few knew it as well as Smith.

Smith's hounds always traveled in couples, literally coupled together with double collars, an arrangement intended to prevent any single hound from running off into the dying night to hunt with or without his fellows. Every hunt trains their puppies by coupling a young hound to an older one to teach the pup to stick with his mates, which is why foxhounds young and old are counted in couples. Smith also used the coupling collars whenever his hounds traveled from place to place, a practice that represented and produced just the kind of chaos that Alexander Henry Higginson found so repugnant in these "so called" American foxhounds. Unruly, barely trained, wild things tugging against one other to be free, they could not be trusted to travel without the coupling collars. It was the only way to maintain any semblance of control. But that's the way Smith liked them. They were intuitive, impulsive, and independent and they showed initiative—like any full-blooded American.

Smith had sent Ham Jackson ahead to scout the creek. The rest of the hunting party trotted down the Turnpike and took a left onto the old lane to Welbourne with the wind at their backs. Not a good sign for hunting again today. Again, no dew; again, too windy. After crossing Panther Skin Creek at the ford, they reached Welbourne within a quarter of an hour. The meet was scheduled for daybreak, 6:38 a.m., and Smith intended to be there ahead of time to cast his hounds as soon as possible. They continued down Welbourne Road past the Pot House and on toward Beaverdam Creek. As they went along they picked up riders hacking to the meet until they reached Leithton Manor, where Higginson's crowd had gathered. The followers numbered near forty that day, half in scarlet, half in black and grey. Those in pink, billeted five miles down the turnpike in Middleburg, were for the English; the others, most of whom lived in the vicinity of Upperville, were for the Americans. Each rider attempted to greet the Master with a "good morning, Master" as is customary in England. Smith just nodded.

"Everyone here?" Smith asked Higginson.

"Yes. My people are here," Higginson said as he watched Smith's hounds practically rioting to get out of their collars.

"Let's be off, then," Smith said. And off they were. No ceremony, no announcements, no stirrup cups of brandy. Time to hunt. At seven minutes past the appointed time, in a covert near the creek back of Leithton Manor, Smith asked his second whip, Claude Hatcher, to dismount and uncouple the hounds. Away they went in a burst so rapid that they were out of sight within seconds. Mal Richardson, Smith's first whip, took the first stone wall into a pasture full of cows on his horse "St. Michael." The horse took off too soon, landed hard on the other side and checked suddenly, sending Richardson flying, but he kept hold of the reins, tucked and rolled when he hit the ground, jumped to his feet, and vaulted back aboard. Hatcher and the hounds were already taking the next wall on the far side of the pasture. They were not seen or heard for the next two hours.

One, two, three flights of rail fences separating fields of mown wheat, corn, and hay met the riders as they took off, trying to find the pack. Both Morley Davis and Higginson's friend Leonard Ahl fell off their horses trying to negotiate these obstacles. Neither were hurt. Next they faced an in-and-out of two stone walls lining an old lane with not much more than a bounce between, and within minutes they faced a hard drop over another rail fence at the road to Unison. This sort of sport resembled a steeplechase rather than a fine English foxhunt, which is just what Harry Worcester Smith intended. After more than thirty minutes of hard galloping and jumping, the field pulled up on the crest of Steptoe Hill overlooking the watershed, their horses blowing hard, steam rising from their hides.

Mrs. Pierce circled her horse, "Bruce," to let him cool gradually. Though he was as fit as any horse out, he was winded and hung his head slightly to gulp air through his flared nostrils. Five ladies were riding aside in the field that morning, circling their horses between the black- and red-coated gentlemen's. Mrs. Davis' horse, "O.K.," a gorgeous dark bay, glistened morning light, the sun having only just gotten high enough to fully light the landscape. Down in the still-dim creek valley a great horned owl took flight upstream. A groundhog dove for cover on the next hillock over. In the exhilaration of the moment there was quite a bit of chatter among the riders and not a little relief expressed for having just survived such a burst of danger. Each rider is fully aware that there are not only human athletes with human attributes and personalities on this remote hillside early on this November morning, but equally varied equine athletes with equally unique personalities and capabilities, faults, and talents. Each team of horse and rider is a separate entity that, in order to negotiate this kind of sport, must be paired mentally and physically to succeed and survive. The giddy atmosphere was almost celebratory, and the day had only just begun.

"Shhhh," Smith commanded the crowd, trying to locate his pack; it was out of sight and possibly out of hearing distance already. He needed quiet, to listen.

Smith, in his black wool coat with grey collar, his spit-shined black boots, and his curly light-brown hair visible at the edges of his hunting cap, commanded the esteem of the field, not with any forbearance, but with a simple aspect of knowledge coupled to an abundance of charisma. He was not a tolerant man, nor did he observe self-restraint. He knew that he could outride and outwit every man, and of course woman, out here. This was his domain and kingdom. He was Master *and* huntsman. Funnily enough, because his burst and flattened lung did not permit him enough air to blow a hunting horn, he carried a whistle around his neck. He had trained his hounds to his whistle just as Cotesworth had trained Higginson's to the horn. He had every confidence in Hatcher and Ham to keep up with the pack. He wanted to stay with the judges to make sure they saw what he saw: the brilliance of his hounds.

Higginson, on his favorite hunter, an aging mare named "All's Well" which he had left behind in Massachusetts but had had to have shipped down to Virginia at the beginning of the week because of his injuries and because she was the safest horse in his barn, stayed well away from Smith on the hilltop. He smiled to himself, knowing the difficulty of judging a contest in which the contestants were essentially invisible. These American hounds might as well be coyotes for all the sophistication they showed. Watching Smith sit slumped, practically slouching in his saddle, Higginson squared his red-clad shoulders and straightened his Roman-nosed profile.

Bob Cotesworth, who hadn't wanted to come out in the first place, stepped his horse "Nugent" next to Higginson's and said, "I'm going in." Allen Potts, the newspaperman not averse to eavesdropping, saw the look of disgust on Cotesworth's face and heard him say, "I've got more important business at home," meaning their temporary quarters in Middleburg. Higginson nodded to dismiss his servant and smiled at Mrs. Pierce, who was never far from Higginson's side.

There they stood spread across the hilltop for ten minutes or more, listening for a trace of a hound's voice. Virginians were used to seeing foxhunters on hilltops every fall. That sort of thing had been going on for years around here. But this band of happy hunters was different. An intensity of contest and stiffness of challenge blew in the breeze. Nothing like a good fight to keep the blood going, Smith thought.

"We can't very well judge them if we can't see them," Dr. McEachran said to Smith.

"Well then let's find them," Smith said wheeling The Cad and galloping off.

At the bottom of the hill near the ford at Hickory Lane, Marguerite and Morley Davis took a wall beautifully in tandem followed by a similar display of horsemanship from Miss Dulany and her cousin Miss Lemmon. Close behind came Higginson and his friend Mr. Ahl on "Tapps," one of seven horses he'd shipped from Massachusetts for The Match. Tapps clipped a front hoof on the wall and unseated Mr. Higginson's friend, who came up scratched but unbroken and on they went.

No hounds at the next covert, the next and the next. No sight of them. On another hill-top: a vacant valley below. All the way to Hogback Mountain near Leesburg, some twenty miles from the meet, they galloped and jumped and galloped after the Grafton pack. Smith, though he knew Hatcher and Ham could and would keep up, was getting a little desperate to find his run-away hounds.

Finally, finally, around nine o'clock—over two hours after the meet—Smith heard his hounds howling in the distance near Marble Quarry as if they'd taken a fox and his heart swelled. He found them near the base of Hogback Mountain—all six and a half couple in good health and spirits, tongues hanging, happy hounds. Smith jumped down to congratulate them, tooting his whistle and rubbing their muzzles. "Good boy Sinner. Good boy Spic. Simple, Simple my boy. Good dogs." Some hounds find, some follow, some chase. Smith knew that these three, his best chasers, had undoubtedly been in the front.

"They got up a red back at Turkey Roost. Four and a half couple stuck with him and chased him to ground here. You can ask these darkies," Hatcher said, indicating three people, a man and two women, standing next to Ham, who was on his pony nearby.

"Yes, sir," they each agreed. "That fox saw them coming and in he went. He was one tired fox," the man said.

"Oh for God's sake," Higginson said. "Why should we believe these people?"

"You can believe them," Smith said fiercely.

Higginson scoffed. "Did your whip see the fox to ground?" he asked Smith.

Hatcher shook his head no. "But they did," he said.

"Again," Dr. McEachran said, "We can't very well judge them if we can't see them working."

"We can believe the whips and the observers," Jim Maddux said.

"What say you, Hal?" Smith asked Hal Movius. Movius stalled, not appreciating the pressure to make a snap judgment. He agreed with both of the other judges, that they hadn't seen the event and that they could believe the witnesses. "The judges will take all into consideration this afternoon at our daily meeting. You should write it in a letter and submit it to the panel."

Smith mounted and blew his whistle for another cast. "Let's take them down toward Mountville on the other side of Snickersville Pike," he said to Hatcher. "Stay close to the creek." The hounds went helter-skelter in the same general direction as their Master and his whips, veering off at will toward whatever small scent they could catch. A deer or two fled the advancing field; the hounds knew their prey and did not chase.

"You can hardly call them a pack," Mrs. Pierce said to Higginson as they trailed behind.

"They're delinquents."

"By God they can run," McEachran said.

"Yes, but where?" Higginson said.

They skirted Mt. Gilead and forded Goose Creek at Hickory Lane again, making their way south by southwest when Smith blew his whistle to cast them into a covert on the south side of Beaverdam. Sinner, the lead hound, gave tongue, if a little reluctantly. Smith encouraged him with an "at-a-boy." Simple, about twenty yards away, chimed in. Nothing definite. Slowly, almost laboriously, the hounds worked for another hour and a half up the creek bed toward the bridge near Mountville.

Reluctantly Smith agreed with Hatcher that they should call it a day. It was almost noon. Smith believed his hounds had shown their grit and most especially their speed. For him the whole point in the match was to show the naysayers that speed was essential in a hound, any hound, that wanted to hunt in America where the foxes, feeding on mice, rabbits, frogs, any damn thing they could find, were wild foxes and not the slow, fat, semi-domesticated foxes that lived in the English countryside feeding on tame pheasants, chickens, and lambs.

Hatcher coupled the hounds again and everyone set out for home, toward Middleburg or Upperville, at least a ten-mile walk in either case. The Upperville group, walking west toward the road to Welbourne, came to a gap in a fence line and, attempting to reach the road on the other side, scrambled up an embankment one by one to the roadbed. When it came Terry Dulany's turn "Bachelor," by this time quite fatigued, slipped a hind leg backward down the embankment where it became entangled in an old spiral of wire hiding in the brush. The horse panicked, feeling trapped, and yanked his foot free with tremendous force, sending the young woman off over his rear end. Falling from a sidesaddle is no fun. Falling from any horse is no fun; from a sidesaddle it is a particularly complicated process what with the upper lower pommel and the leaping head and the single stirrup all designed to keep a girl securely seated while jumping, not falling. Luckily she was not hurt and made it back to Welbourne safely. When she told her grandfather what had happened he sent a brigade of men out across the countryside to cut and ribbon any and all wire fences in places suitable for jumping, allowing safer riding for the remainder of the two-week Match.

Harry Worcester Smith submitted the following letter to the judges that afternoon:

"Allen Potts, Esq., Clerk of the Match:
Dear Sir—I would ask that the judges give the Grafton Pack credit for the work done this morning in finding, starting and running a red fox from about the Leithton Plantations to the Marble Quarry. Testimonials may be received from Mrs. Henderson of Clarke [County], who rode in today, and inhabitants of the house at Marble Quarry. Also Claude Hatcher, who was one of the parties who found the hounds at the Marble Quarry.

Yours Truly,
Harry W. Smith
M.F.H. Grafton Hunt"[2]

Alexander Henry Higginson (1876–1958)

ALEXANDER HENRY HIGGINSON WAS A HORSE OF A DIFFERENT COLOR. He was a Harvard man, a Brahmin of Puritan and Unitarian stock. He tried science, but put it aside; thought of business, but no. He was, above all else, exclusively, a foxhunter. Beginning in his late teens, foxhunting became his passion, his avocation, his vocation. "We all have hobbies," he writes in the Preface to an unpublished manuscript. "Mine is foxhunting. I think of it, dream of it, talk of it all the time."[1] He took it on, not only as a gentleman's pastime, but as a mantle, an identity, a persona. He was *the* gentleman foxhunter. He didn't dabble; he dove: scarlet jacket, cordovan-topped boots, top hat, bone-handled whip—he is rarely pictured without his costume. He called his servants with a silver horn; his house was the kind of house "where the walls and book cases call the foxhunter."[2] Beginning with his pack of drag-hunt beagles in the late 1890s, he spent his life among horses, hounds, and the people who follow them and, though he later lamented his involvement in The Match, he dedicated his life to what he considered the best foxhounds the world over: the English hound. When he died his library contained, exclusively, volumes concerning British foxhounds and foxhunting. Americans be damned.

"In the fall of 1883," Alexander Henry Higginson begins his auto-biography, *Try Back* (1931), "I was taken by my father to see a meet of the Myopia Hounds at the Gibney Farm at Hamilton, Massachusetts. . . . I was old enough to have a pony, and I remember well that my cup of happiness was well-nigh overflowing when my father allowed me to go to a meet mounted." Alexander was interested in yachting for a time, but that didn't stick, nor did mountain climbing. "My father said to me,"

Higginson writes in *An Old Sportsman's Memories*, his 1951 autobiography, "You're not lazy, and I know you're not vicious, though you are terribly extravagant.... I can see that you work at your sport.... I'll build you a better house and you can lead the life of a country gentleman ... *there are not many of those in America* ... you don't drink, you don't gamble and you don't keep a mistress."[3] At twenty-eight he was bankrolled and backed, set up and secured on his very own estate with mansion, stables, kennels, and servants in the town of South Lincoln just west of Boston on a hilltop near Walden Pond. He called his new estate Middlesex Meadows and his hunt, bound by Foxboro and Groton in the west, Clematis Brook in the east, the Norfolk County Hunt territory in the south, and Billerica in the north, was the Middlesex Hunt.

How does the son of a much-admired, even heroic man turn to foxhunting for fulfillment? Throughout the many thousands of words A. H. Higginson wrote during his life about the sport and its Masters, he never exhibits a tone of braggadocio, nor does he write, like so many others, with the intention of turning the sport into a heroic effort of monumental importance. He just loved to hunt. He loved hounds and horses, and once he set out to master it, though it took a lifetime, he very carefully, methodically did indeed master it.

Alexander's father, Henry Lee Higginson, and his mother, Ida Agassiz Higginson, were pillars of Boston's financial and cultural society. They weren't a foxhunting family, but then very few were at that time in America. Indeed, Alexander was the tenth direct paternal descendant of men who had founded New England, forged the Constitution, fought to preserve the Union, enriched her as merchants and financiers, and seen beyond to establish her deeper cultural institutions for the betterment of her soul. Maybe it was the very weight of all those generations of great men and women, the shadow of the famous, maybe it was watching, listening, and learning about the hardships and heartbreak that invariably attend a father's work, the work of a visionary, that induced the son to chuck it and retreat west for the peace of the countryside. Countryside he got; peace not so much. His Match against Harry Worcester Smith haunted him for the rest of his life.

The Reverend Francis was the first Higginson to step ashore in the Colonies in 1629, part of the tribe of nonconformists in The Great Migration, where, in Francis's own words: "the Lord stirred up the spirits of so many thousands of his servants, to leave the *pleasant land* of England, the land of their *nativity*, and to transport themselves, and their families, over the *ocean sea*, into the *desert land* of America, . . . in a place where time out of mind, had been nothing before but *Heathenism, Idolotry, and Devil-worship*.[4] Though he only lived a year in the Colonies—Francis died of a fever in 1630 at the age of forty-three—he led a fleet of six ships and, along with wife and their eight children, was among the 350 passengers, including cattle, horses, sheep, goats, and hogs, in the first wave of the Massachusetts Bay Colony that set Salem on its famous and infamous course. Francis writes in his diary of the settlement, *New Englands Plantation*, "It is scarce to be believed how our Kine and Goats, Horses and Hogges doe thriue and prosper here and like well this Countrey."

When Francis died, his son John took over as Salem's minister, where he preached for the next fifty years. Cotton Mather called John "the first in a catalogue of heroes."[5] John Higginson wrote the Attestation to Mather's *Magnalia Chirsti Americana*. His daughter Ann Dolliver was accused but never brought to trial in Salem's 1683 witch trials.[6] John was sixty-seven at the time. Ann Dolliver's husband had abandoned her and her children and she had returned home to live with her father. John later wrote the Preface to John Hale's *A Modest Inquiry into the Nature of Witchcraft*, in which he more or less apologizes for the whole affair.

Skip a few generations of clergymen, seamen, soldiers, administrators, and merchants and we come to Alexander's more immediate influences: Stephen, George, and Henry Lee Higginson. Stephen Higginson, Alexander's great-grandfather, was a ship owner and Massachusetts delegate to the Constitutional Congress in 1783. He hated Thomas Jefferson and was a member of the Essex Junto, author of *The Writings of Laco*—a denunciation of John Hancock's campaign for governor of Massachusetts in 1789—"an arch conservative and elitist."[7] Stephen's son George, Alexander's grandfather, was also a merchant, "a stanch Whig and Unitarian, admirer of Emerson and reader of Dickens and Thackery . . . a glorious example of the English virtue of somehow 'winning through.'"[8] When incorrectly assessed for his taxes (on the low side), George insisted in paying double what was owed. Alexander's cousin (once removed) was the redoubtable abolitionist Thomas Wentworth Higginson, one of the leaders of some fifty thousand demonstrators in a march through Boston against the shipment of Anthony Burns, the last fugitive slave to be returned under the Fugitive Slave Act, back to the South. Later Wentworth commanded the first Union regiment of black soldiers in the Civil War. Henry Lee Higginson, Alexander's father, was a "stiff-backed patrician, a democratic philanthropist whose integrity and warmth were signatures of his success."[9] The Higginsons were related by marriage to the Cabots, Jacksons, Lowells, Channings, Perkinses, Tyngs, Storrows, Putnums, Morses, and Paines; throughout the generations they proved themselves a "prolific, generous, stubborn race, not slow to wrath, and honest as the sunlight . . . piety, courage, beneficence, patriotism, and a keen sense of personal honor were the traditions of the house."[10]

Within the generation of Higginsons that straddled the turn of the twentieth century, Henry Lee and his older cousin (Thomas) Wentworth Higginson, the mood shifted, the load of Puritanism lifted, and the Higginsons rejoiced in the Enlightenment. Wentworth, the abolitionist, was also Wentworth the would-be poet who "inhabited the sunny side of transcendentalism—idealists who routed Puritan gloom depravity and sin."[11] At the time, Ralph Waldo Emerson had been disinvited from speaking ever again at Harvard for preaching that "God incarnates himself in man," and Henry Adams asked for educational reform out in the open—on the playground, in the light of day. America's Renaissance, her happy fin de siècle, included love of nature and humanity: Good things can come from reform; pessimism was out the door. Wentworth befriended his neighbor, the reclusive Emily Dickenson, edited her poems, and encouraged her to write, including her "typographical eccentricities," though very few were published in her lifetime.[12] Henry Lee Higginson became one of Boston's leading philanthropists, founded her symphony orchestra, endowed her democratic endeavors, nurtured her soul. Henry Lee and Wentworth may have inherited a conscience, but neither mistook it for moderation.

Henry Lee was perhaps the epitome of the Higginson "race." He was a meliorist—he believed that human effort would make the world a better place. While upholding the Brahmin standards of urbane philanthropy, courageous self-determination, and that of marrying into other Brahmin families—in his case the Lees—Henry Lee Higginson came of age, not in Boston among his fellows at Harvard, but in Europe where music captured his soul. No Higginson since Francis had attended college, but Henry, like all of his family's friends, relatives, and acquaintances, was expected to attend Boston Latin School and Harvard College. In the 1840s Boston Latin School was a Dickensian relic, "an ugly one-story brick building, with granite façade . . . noisy street, no playground, dark stairs, ventilation wretched . . . its methods bad, its standards low, its rooms unspeakably gloomy, where teachers lacked nobility and generosity."[13] Poor little boys. Never fear, on to Harvard. But because he had very bad eyes and could not keep up with the heavy reading schedule demanded at Harvard, Henry Lee was allowed to leave after his first year. In those days, the next best thing to Harvard was Europe, and he was permitted to escape Boston's eighteenth-century atmosphere for a walking tour, a Grand Tour, of Europe.

He and his companion, an older clergyman, began with a walk through Switzerland during which he wrote to his friend Alexander Agassiz, whose father Louis was the famous Swiss glaciologist and Harvard's preeminent naturalist, that he had stood on the Aar glacier, near Dr. Agassiz's hut. The Agassizs' and Higginsons' futures were destined to intertwine, but first Henry Lee wanted to fill his heart and mind with music. He and the clergyman parted ways so that Henry Lee could spend weeks and months in London, Milan, Munich, Dresden, and later two years in Vienna studying harmony, voice, and piano—living and breathing opera. "I think I should stay here," he wrote home, "and learn what I can with my ears." Much later, in his eighties when he dictated his memoirs, he looked back without regret for not having received a Harvard education. "Harvard boys, failed then, as they have failed in so many college generations since, to lift up their eyes to new horizons of the mind and spirit."[14] Like many late-nineteenth-century Americans, he came to believe that music "mined deeper truths than words or pictures," and though he found that his musical studies flew against his "Yankee pragmatism," in the end he learned to "combine pragmatism and idealism in equal measure."[15]

Shortly before the Civil War broke out, Henry Lee Higginson returned to Boston. He was twenty-six when he joined first the 2nd Massachusetts Regiment and then the 1st Massachusetts Cavalry in the Army of the Potomac. His letters home those first weeks in training at Camp Meigs in Readville, Massachusetts, prove the mixture of naïvety and pride of purpose of a new recruit. "Now I ride around on a big horse. I have *two* rows of brass buttons on my coat . . . and am generally just as big as I can swell."[16] His years in Europe had helped his resolve: "my whole belief and hope in everything, in life, in man, in woman, in music, in good, in the beautiful, in the real truth rests on the question now before us."[17] In Europe he had been told "there is no American people, no nationality, is no distinct and strong love of country."[18] He was prepared to disagree. He served alongside Charles Francis Adams Jr., grandson and great-grandson of two presidents; Robert Gould Shaw, commander of the 54th Massachusetts Infantry Regiment of black soldiers; Oliver Wendell Holmes Jr., future Supreme Court justice; and his special friend Charles Russell Lowell, who was killed at the Battle of Cedar Creek in the Shenandoah Valley Campaign. He also understood the conflicting sentiments in his hometown. "Very many people whom we naturally saw, old and young in Boston, were interested in cotton manufacturers and had many friends in the South, and did not share the strong feelings that [his family] held about slavery."[19] Henry Lee was never conflicted; war, in his opinion, made the man. "I do thank God that I never had but one feeling about the war, pure and undivided from the first," he writes in his war diary, "I always did long for some such war, and it came in the nick of time for me."

A horseman Henry Lee was not—at least not in the beginning. At the outset of the Civil War the Northern cavalry recruits were sorely mismatched to their Southern counterparts. The Union had no cavalry bureau at Washington, no general in command of a cavalry unit, and "no Federal officer of high rank in the field seemed to understand the proper use of mounted troops . . . they were wasted and demoralized, frittered away on random futilities."[20] "I was ignorant as a baby about horses when

I joined the regiment at Readsville," Henry wrote home. Like everything he did, he was dedicated, learned quickly, and soon acquired the title he kept the rest of his life: Major Henry Lee Higginson. He found a passion for horses during the war, undoubtedly fed by the realization of what a willing horse will do and become if asked by a human. His War Horses included "Rats," "Piggy," "Nutmeg," and "Grater."

And here's the weird coincidence: forty years *before* Alexander Henry Higginson's Great Hound Match, his father had his own, though much more dire, match not five miles from Middleburg, indeed across the very territory that eventually became so familiar to the son. On June 17, 1863, though he had survived Ambrose Burnside's bungled command at Antietam and cowardly Hooker's at Chancellorsville, Henry Lee Higginson found himself in Aldie, Virginia, just east of Middleburg on what is now called Mosby's Highway. "A very beautiful country indeed," he had written home the week before, while riding north through the Piedmont on J. E. B. Stuart's trail. "The grass is wonderfully green, the slopes from hill to valley are beautiful . . . the houses are quite fine and very stately."[21] Aldie, a village in a strategic gap between the Bull Run and Catoctin Mountains on the Little River, was the home territory of John Mosby's guerrilla Raiders and J. E. B. Stuart's Army of Northern Virginia. The Battle of Brandy Station, which had taken place the previous week, the first in the Gettysburg campaign, had proven the northern cavalry finally up to the South's challenge. Henry Lee Higginson had just received a new horse, a big gray, since his "Nutmeg" had gone lame. The 1st Massachusetts was finally gaining confidence in themselves as cavalrymen; the battle of Brandy Station had proven them competent in their saddles. When they came clattering into the village of Aldie, Major Higginson and his men were attacked by the Fifth Virginia cavalry under Colonel Rosser, a favorite of Stuart's. Major Henry Lee was wounded in hand-to-hand combat, his horse was shot four times, the Major fell and lay on the road "with a sabre-cut across his face and a pistol bullet at the base of his spine."[22]

Thus were the Higginsons introduced to Virginia's Piedmont. Henry Lee was sent home to recover while his friends marched on to Gettysburg. Though the Major survived his wounds, because of their severity, he only returned to battle briefly in 1864. His horse, taken by the Confederates, was recovered and remained the Major's riding horse for many years. He was promoted to Brevet Lieutenant Colonel, but was always known as Major. He lost many friends and neighbors whom he never forgot and would later honor with his gift of "Soldiers Field" to Harvard in 1890. While recovering in Boston, he married Ida Agassiz.

She must have been a real breath of air to the wounded soldier. She came from a family of naturalists; her father was Louis Agassiz, the glaciologist whom Henry Lee had written home about from Europe. Ida's brother, Alexander, was a good friend and classmate of Henry Lee's. Her childhood home, on Quincy Street in Boston, was "as much a home for animals as for the family."[23] Louis was head of Harvard's Lawrence Scientific School and founded its Museum of Comparative Zoology. Any overflowing specimens were kept in jars of alcohol in a wooden shed that the neighbors called "Zoological Hall" in the Agassizs' backyard, where the fear of fire was ever present. There was also a hutch of rabbits, possibly to feed the pair of eagles, and the bear cub named Bruin, who broke free one evening and joined a dinner party at the dining table. Visitors to the professor's house included Charles Eliot Norton, professor of poetry at Harvard, Henry Wadsworth Longfellow, Charles Sumner, Edward Prince of Wales, Prince Napoleon III and his consort, the pianist Sigismond Thalberg, Charles Dickens, and William Makepeace Thackeray. Napoleon had offered Professor Agassiz the chair of zoology at *Jardins de Plantes*, but he declined "for the love of science and its possibilities in the New World."[24]

Ida's stepmother, Elizabeth Cabot (nee Cary) was also a great naturalist and educator. She was Louis's second wife; his first, Ida's mother, Celcile Braun, had died in Europe. "Lizzy" accompanied her husband Louis on his scientific expeditions to Brazil in 1865, after which she published *A Journey to Brazil*, and they sailed around Cape Horn in 1871. She also assisted her son Alexander, Ida's brother and also a naturalist, in publishing his *Seaside Studies in Natural History* in 1865. When Louis ran into significant financial problems before the Civil War, Lizzy started a school for girls in their home and successfully pulled him out of the mess. Louis died in 1870, after which Lizzy published *Louis Agassiz: His Life and Correspondence*. Louis Agassiz is known today in the history of science, not only for his tremendous contributions to the study of European, South American, and North American natural history, but also for his belief in polygenics, a form of "scientific racism," and for his unrelenting denial of Darwin's theories of evolution and natural selection. "Louis was the last of the great naturalists who believed in the special creation of species and the theological tenants that it implied."[25] Lizzy survived her famous husband; "though she was a facile instrument in the hands of her husband, she never lost her identity in his immense personality."[26] She lived to be a founding member of Radcliff College in 1879, where she served as president until 1902, pushing for "granting to the students the same courses as were offered at Harvard and by the same instructors." She retired at seventy-two.

Coming from such a distinguished, gutsy family, Ida could only have been just what Henry Lee needed to heal his war injuries. After the war, he and Ida took part in The Great Experiment of Reconstruction—the resettlement of the South with former slaves as paid farm laborers. With a group of investors, they bought a five-thousand-acre Georgia cotton plantation called "Cottonham," including a house, stables, and former slave quarters for $30,000. It had been decimated by Sherman's fire brigade. Nevertheless, Henry Lee and Ida moved south in good faith that they could revise and revive. As W. E. B. DuBois said of other Northerners like the Higginsons, "To [them] the Southern problem is simply that of making efficient working men out of this material [former slaves], by giving them the requisite technical skill and the help of invested capital."[27]

The Higginsons put their heart into the scheme for one year, Ida teaching school to children her father had deemed biologically inferior, and Henry trying to bring in a cotton harvest. They paid each married couple $370 per year and gave them a house and two acres of land on which to subsist. Ida wrote her impressions in a diary, at first describing the newly liberated workers as "good, active, honest people," but later they became "curious creatures, unable to work on their own, very strange with wits and intellect far ahead of their morals." Henry could not understand why the former slaves expected "to be fed and cared for." He said the "darkies" could learn and comprehend quickly but were deficient in "moral character." After a year, the Higginsons gave up and sold the place at a loss to the investors of $65,000.[28] "We were glad to be rid of it," Henry Lee said later.

He returned home, $10,000 in debt and was taken into his father George's brokerage house, Lee, Higginson and Company, "as a matter of charity, to keep me out of the poor house," he later wrote.[29] One of the firm's chief interests was the Calumet and Hecla Copper mine, a lode of verdigris copper in the Calumet conglomerate on the Keweenaw Peninsula in Northern Michigan. Alexander Agassiz was now Henry Lee's brother-in-law, a practicing geologist and an investor in the mine. He brought it out of bankruptcy into solvency, using Lee, Higginson and Company as the mine's bank and brokerage house. Originally selling for five dollars a share, of which Henry Lee, his brothers, and his father, George, had bought as many as they could afford, by 1909 the stock was worth a thousand a share.

Henry Lee Higginson "saw the world as a better place than it proved to be." His optimism led him to become one of Boston's best-remembered philanthropists. His biographer, Bliss Perry, called him "a curiously subtle combination of warrior and philosopher . . . picturesque, ejaculating, intimate, illogical, noble, whimsical, reckless delightful."[30] In 1881 he founded the Boston Symphony Orchestra, building Symphony Hall in 1900. He was awarded an honorary MA from Harvard in 1882 and proceeded to give the school thirty-one acres on which to build Soldier's Field, dedicating it to Charlie Lowell, his good friend who had fallen near the Shenandoah. Charlie had once admonished Henry Lee to "become a useful citizen . . . a mighty unpretending hero." Henry Lee also donated the Harvard Union "to democratize campus, so that rich and poor can stand on footing equal in all respects."

In 1875 Henry Lee and Ida Higginson's only child, Cecile, died at the age of five. Henry Lee was forty-two and Ida was nearly forty. Alexander was born a year later, April 2, 1876. Thereafter, "the yearning solicitude of the father followed every waking and sleeping instant of the boy's life."[31] His mother called him "Sonny." His early education was under tutors in Boston and at a school run by a friend of his father's, John P. Hopkinson, on Chestnut Street. His class at Harvard was that of 1898 and following graduation he took several postgraduate classes in ornithology. Possibly as a nod to his grandfather Agassiz, Alexander tried life as a "man of science." In May of 1898 he made an expedition, financed by his father, to Texas, New Mexico, and into northern California with Clinton Hart Merriam, head of the US Biological Survey—predecessor of the US Fish and Wildlife Service—and one of the original founders of the National Geographic Society, along with Vernon Bailey, chief field naturalist for the survey. Higginson wrote to his fiancée, Rosamond Tudor, from the expedition: "I'm afraid you're going to be disappointed with me when we meet, for to judge by your letters, you seem to take it for granted that I have changed; and that I take a more serious view of life. I *don't*. I still like my hounds and my yachting."[32] Rosamond, an accomplished artist having trained at the Boston Museum of Fine Arts, and Higginson were married that winter while the Boston Symphony Orchestra played the wedding march. Together, they spent the following winter in Montana on another ornithological expedition to Staunton Lake just off the Great Northern Railway, where they lived in an eighteen-by-twenty-four-foot log cabin. "It was quite an absorbing experience for a woman who was unused to the woods," Higginson writes in *An Old Sportsman's Memoirs*. He neglects to mention that his wife was pregnant that winter. He does say that she "painted birds." They were divorced in 1902 when she fell in love with one of Higginson's childhood friends, William Starling Burgess, a naval architect who was designing a yacht for Higginson.

He also tried life as a financier in his father and grandfather's firm, Lee, Higginson and Co. Then, after he survived a bout of typhoid fever in 1903, Alexander's father agreed to set him up in the country, buy him a string of hunters and some hounds, and build a house and kennels for him. In his memoir *Try Back*, Alexander writes "my father was the kindest man in the world . . . it seemed as if nothing Father could do for me was too much."

A half-century after Henry Lee Higginson wrote home in defense of America, admonishing those Europeans who had said, "there is no America, no nationality," his son Alexander wrote a letter to *Rider and Driver* in a very different vein: "There is no American hound," he declared, only "chance-bred" mutts. When George Bernard Shaw's play

Pygmalion was published in 1912, Harry Worcester Smith may have wondered if Shaw's character Professor Henry Higgins was based on Smith's rival Alexander Henry Higginson: an Englishman more English than an Englishman. Where was his national pride, his sense of honor? In England . . . where else?

8

Day Three

Friday, November 3, 1905
Middlesex Hunt's Second

"No finer sight can be imagined than that of eighteen and a half couple of perfectly matched hounds flying over the hills and down through the valleys that make Piedmont Valley the greatest hunting section in the country."

—ALLEN POTTS, *RICHMOND TIMES DISPATCH*, FRIDAY, NOVEMBER 4, 1905

"There they go!"

"Would you look at that—"

"Ain't that something?"

Spectators lined the stone bridge over Goose Creek looking north into the Dulany's fields at Lemmon's Bottom. Eighteen and a half couple of stout strong English hounds were screaming across a hillside in the distance in full cry. Gone Away.

"Beautiful."

Masters, huntsmen, whips, hounds, and followers on horseback, in buggies, and on foot had met once again at daybreak at the bridge to witness Master Higginson's second chance to win the two-thousand-dollar prize for killing a fox in Virginia.

"Fred Okie is acting as judge today and tomorrow in place of Jim Maddux," Higginson reminded Cotesworth.

"He'd be best to keep up," Cotesworth said. "I'm not in the mood to mollycoddle some clodhopper."

"Just be aware of the judges," Higginson said.

"Sir," Cotesworth said, clipping the word with a short inhalation as though he'd gasped the title.

Today Higginson, Cotesworth, and the whips had arrived together and on time and, though Higginson's ribs were still wrapped, he had slept well in his feather bed at Mrs. Brown's abode after a truly wonderful dinner of fresh venison and new potatoes, "the last of the green beans," as she had told the crowded dinner table, and a fine apple pudding. The Middlesex party had settled in nicely at Mrs. Brown's, growing accustomed to the sketchy sleeping arrangements; the rooms had to be divided with screens to accommodate the whole party, and the outdoor toilet augmented with an abundance of chamber pots. Mrs. Brown was an excellent cook and for a hungry group of hunters, that was the main concern. Everything else was gravy.

Conditions had not much changed overnight. Although clouds had moved in to make the morning overcast, the breeze was still problematic. Cotesworth's first cast was across Panther Skin Creek in a practically fallow field of weeds and stubble back of Welbourne. Higginson's lead hounds "Visitor" and "Vigilance" began to whimper almost immediately, but stopped as soon as they had started. Cotesworth, on his hack homeward the day before, had come through this very field and seen three foxes—a vixen, a grown cub, and a dog fox—at regular intervals along Panther Skin Creek. Despite the lousy conditions again, this morning he figured his hounds could find and chase at least one dog fox. He picked the hounds up with his horn and moved them away up and down the hillocks bit by bit hoping for a cold scent. His good English foxhounds worked hard for more than an hour, finding it blank wherever they ventured. The field was impatient to be off. All were on fresh horses; no single horse can run as hard as these riders demanded day after day. Higginson was on "Owaissa" today and Smith rode "Prosper." Higginson ordered Cotesworth to take the pack across Panther Skin Creek to obtain the east side of Goose Creek closer to Middleburg.

Up the Goose Creek Valley the hounds worked, good, diligent creatures. Higginson loved them all the more with each passing day as he watched them at their jobs. Since the bulk of the pack had only arrived in the States in April, they weren't entirely accustomed to the weather, the seasons, the conditions. Certainly not in Virginia. To be victim to the whims of the weather gods was a foxhunter's plight, like it or not.

"They're working well," Mrs. Pierce said to Higginson, apparently reading his mind.

"Aren't they?"

"No matter the outcome of this thing, Alex, you've shown your hounds in the best light."

"Yes well, I'm not giving up yet. Look at Smith, the smug bastard. He's constantly second-guessing Cotesworth, I can see it on his face."

"Cotesworth doesn't give a hoot what Smith thinks," Mrs. Pierce said.

"He gives more than you think. He's a brooding fellow. Drinks like a fish. If I can keep him off the booze this week, we may win this thing yet."

Even without a run, the field had a fair bit of riding to keep close to the hounds between each covert throughout the morning. This area of Loudoun County is crisscrossed by hundreds of little streams fed by countless springs in the Goose Creek watershed. Though it hadn't rained for several days the creeks were full. The more than thirty riders out again today had plenty of walls and plank or rail fences to negotiate. Then, at a road bed in a remote corner of Colonel Dulany's property, Harry Worcester Smith decided to show the extent of his often less than splendid judgment.

Higginson had jumped a stone wall into the road and trotted down it looking for a place to enter the next field since the fence-line protecting it was not on the Dulany property and was made mostly of wire.

"There's a gate down here," Smith said, trotting ahead of Higginson. "Ham can open it for us." Ham Jackson, not being welcome to ride along with the field, was ever-present in the shadows of the streams and hillsides to be called upon to open a gate whenever necessary.

As if by magic, he came toward them from the opposite direction. "I thought you might need this one opened," he called out to Smith.

Before Jackson could dismount and in front of the crowd as if he were in a high jumping show ring with spectators cheering him on, Smith spurred Prosper toward the gate. It was at least five feet high, a rickety wooden thing not much wider than it was high and hanging loosely from rusty hinges. The approach was from an odd angle and Prosper was only three strides out, the top of the gate being level with his fine withers. He didn't balk or really even blink at his rider's foolish request and took off in a completely honest attempt to jump it without having a really good look at the thing. It was an awkward takeoff. His left forefoot clipped it, he twisted in midair and came down in a heap on the other side. Smith rolled free without getting his leg caught beneath his brave horse, but the horse lay there motionless, dazed.

Horses are breakable. When twelve hundred pounds of horseflesh comes down at the worst possible angle a horse can break its neck, a leg, or its back. The field stood in the road aghast at the nerve of such an unnecessary, really stupid, show of bravado.

"What an idiot," Mrs. Pierce said without attempting to hide her distain.

"Open the goddamn gate," Higginson screamed at Jackson who also stood agape at the scene before him. He did so and stood back as the riders steered their mounts through the narrow passage and around the fallen horse.

Smith tugged on his horse's reins and nudged him with his boot to urge him up again. Still, Prosper lay there, sides heaving.

"I feel like I'm Anna Karenina watching the death of Frau Frau," Mrs. Pierce said.

Higginson jumped down. Just as he reached for the foreleg to check if it was broken, Prosper struggled to his feet like a prize fighter from the mat and shook it off. Higginson remounted his own horse and waved the field forward. "Leave the fool behind," he shouted without waiting for Smith. Smith vaulted on and spurred the good horse forward.

Suddenly Visitor, with a high note of joy, called out to the rest of the pack that he'd found a cold trail. Yes! Here it is, he wailed, it's cold but true! Three more couple gathered near to confirm the find and off they went in full cry down the Goose Creek Valley.

"Good old Visitor," Higginson said, spurring Owaissa after them.

Cotesworth blew "gone away" on his horn, a warbling blast that will wake the countryside and cause a foxhunter's heart to soar.[1] The field took off after Higginson, with Smith once again close on his heels. Cotesworth and the whips gathered the rest of the pack, caught up with the leaders streaming along crying in that lovely chorus that foxhunters call music.

Throughout the morning's work they had traveled almost ten miles farther and farther east; now they were headed back the way they'd come with two creek crossings in the distance. At the confluence of Panther Skin and the much larger Goose Creek, the two streams joined in a wide bottom about sixty yards across, half of that being the creek itself. They wound down Goose Creek with an eye for a crossing. The creek was deep, deeper than it looked, the banks became steeper and the hounds were screaming straight toward it. The fox must have thought carefully where to cross, this being the most likely place to stop them in their fat hound tracks.

In they jumped without pause, the whole pack leaping from the bank one by one and two by two, landing almost halfway across, swimming like champion water-loving Labradors.

"Ha!" Allen Potts said to Mrs. Pierce. "They're singing while they swim!" At least half the hounds paddled hard enough to lift their snouts out of the water and give a good howl or two. Then they scrambled out on the other side to be off once more.

"There's a bridge down here. We can catch them up," a man from Virginia called to the field as he pointed south; most galloped after him, including Higginson and his huntsman. Smith decided to chance a crossing. Allen Potts stuck around to watch.

"Come on, Fred," Smith said to Fred Okie, Jim Maddux's substitute judge, who felt obliged to stay up with the hounds no matter what. "We can cross here and catch up with them."

Okie looked doubtful. Smith smacked Prosper with his stick and kicked him toward the water. Okie did likewise and just as Prosper was about to take the plunge, Okie's horse, to his surprise, took a flying leap into the drink. Smith's horse shied sideways and Smith went off into the mud. Down Okie and his horse went into a deep hole. The small group of riders who had thought of crossing here too watched with horror as neither Okie nor his horse surfaced. For an interminable moment both were underwater with only a swirling whirlpool to mark the spot where they had entered. Then up popped Okie, still on his horse's back, sputtering and kicking the horse toward the far bank.

"Get off of him," one man shouted. "Swim away so he can get his head up!"

Okie dove free and his horse's nose surfaced, nostrils flaring for air. Then his eyes and ears surfaced as he kicked madly for shore. An unexpectedly strong current carried them downstream several yards as both the horse and rider kicked toward the far bank. A low branch grazed the horse's head and sent him under again. Okie grabbed it, still pulling the horse by the reins.

"Let go of him!" the man, who evidently had some experience with this sort of thing, shouted. "He'll manage on his own."

Okie let go and pulled himself along the branch back to the bank where a friend reached down with a helpful hand to pull him up to the roadbed. He'd made landfall about fifteen yards downstream on the same side he'd entered. The horse, untethered to his rider, swam farther downstream and found some good footing on which to pull himself free of the torrent. Okie sat dazed in the road. His horse, dragging his reins, walked up and nudged him to rise and mount as if to say, "come on, they're getting away." As Okie and his friends trotted toward the bridge to safety they came upon Bolling Haxall trying the same stunt in a place he thought shallower and safer to cross. Someone helped Haxall and his horse ashore in a replay of the Okie story.

"We thought you'd drown," a woman said to Okie.

"So did I!" he said. "Where's Smith?"

"Oh he took off a while ago," someone else said. "Left you to fend for yourself."

"I think I'll go in," Okie said. "That's enough for me today."

Later, when Mrs. Pierce heard that Fred Okie had gone in early she said to Higginson, "Some judge he picked," and Higginson replied, "I shouldn't be, but Smith never ceases to amaze me."

After two and a half more hours of fruitless casting up and down Panther Skin Creek, the hounds finally found and ran their fox for forty-five minutes in a straight line back to the Dulany's land, crossing Goose Creek twice, singing all the way. At one point a farmer, through whose farmyard the field had galloped, dropped everything, climbed aboard his cob and took off after them. At the first jump, a four-board plank fence, cob and farmer took flight, farmer came off, and cob kept running.

"Runaway horse!" someone shouted as the big little horse shot straight through the field in an attempt to catch the fox himself or at least win the race.

"Watch out!" another rider yelled as it plowed into a couple of riders in its way, nearly unseating Mrs. Pierce.

"Catch the damn thing," Higginson said and Ham Jackson again appeared from nowhere.

There was a check after a ford at Panther Skin Creek when the hounds lost their fox temporarily, but it was brief and they were soon gone again. They ran across two more fields with jumps between, but a wind kicked up at around eleven o'clock and the scent was lost. Cotesworth tried casting them a few more times in an effort to find again. Though Colonel Dulany had had all the earth stopped on his property the night before, barring the foxes from going to ground, without scent what's the use? At eleven-thirty Higginson called the whole thing off. The fast and clever fox had disappeared. The run was confirmed by two riders, Mr. Roszell and Mr. Garnett, who said that they had been left behind and had seen "Reynard," running ahead of the hounds "bush dragging." Only twelve of the thirty-six riders who had met at daybreak on the Goose Creek Bridge were among those finishing with the hounds at the end.

A few locals had brought a picnic lunch to the Goose Creek Bridge and settled into their buggies to watch the show from afar. They were not disappointed as the day's hunt ended almost where it had begun in the Dulanys' fallow field back of Welbourne. "I've never seen anything like that," a man said, whistling the tune that to all the world, even a Yankee, means "get a load of that!"

9

Land of the Dulanys

US ROUTE 50 IS A TRANSCONTINENTAL HIGHWAY FROM SACRAMENTO, California, to Ocean City, Maryland. Originally an Indian trail and then part of Colonial and early America's turnpike system, today it crosses the Loudoun Valley in northern Virginia like a sine wave given off by the Alleghany Mountains on its way to the Atlantic—now in Loudoun County, now in Fauquier, back to Loudoun—it sounds a beautiful ground swell of fertility: This is rich, this is green, this is Virginia's Hunt Country.

Harry Worcester Smith "discovered" Hunt Country in 1898, much like white people "discovered" the Americas. The Shenandoah Valley, one of the only natural prairies on the Atlantic Seaboard and a coveted hunting ground, first for the Sioux and then the Iroquois Nations, was home to elk, deer, bear, wolf, and the native grey fox. European foxhunters had peopled colonial Virginia, riding across the exquisitely rolling blue-ridged country all the way back to Thomas, the 6th Lord Fairfax of Cameron, who inherited the whole of the Potomac watershed—some five million acres called the Northern Neck Proprietary—and immigrated to the Shenandoah Valley in 1747. He brought with him a few English hounds to hunt with his young friend George Washington. European settlers in the Piedmont acquired huge parcels of land through Lord Fairfax's Northern Neck Proprietary. With all that land, all those horses, their English traditions, and plenty of leisure time due to slave labor, Colonial Virginians and their descendants almost inevitably became foxhunters. They had swapped, crossbred, and purified the Virginia hound long before the Yankees arrived from New England.

Then Harry came—he saw—and he said it was good.

Rich bluegrass pasture lands, the Shenandoah Valley and the Piedmont are Virginia's feathered cap protruding northeast, allowing the Potomac to carve her natural northern border. Northern Virginia was never part of the Cotton Belt—the Black Belt, as it was known to Booker T. Washington and later W. E. B. Dubois—which snaked through southern Virginia across the Carolinas and deeper south toward the Gulf before and after the American Revolution. Many families in Loudoun and Fauquier Counties did hold slaves, though fewer than the Cotton Belt plantations. When Harry visited the Loudoun Valley in the late 1890s he was the guest of the Dulanys, a former slave-holding family with deep financial ties in the North, where the Dulany children were educated.

"I went to the Piedmont country, near Upperville, Virginia," Smith writes in his unpublished autobiography, "as the guest of H. Rozier Dulany. I at once saw the opportunity of establishing hounds and hunting in what I felt was the best hunting country in the United States, and, if the sport which I anticipated could be shown, that it would not be long before lovers of the chase would come from the North and, choosing their domiciles, learn to love the Old Dominion with its courtesies, kindnesses and carefree ways."[1] Smith never imagined anything small. A grand scheme ensued: establish the American foxhound as a separate and distinct breed while establishing Loudoun and Fauquier counties as the "American Leicester."

The Dulany family seat was at "Welbourne" on what was originally a two-thousand-acre tract in southwest Loudoun County. Seventy-eight-year-old Richard Henry Dulany, uncle of the aforementioned H. Rozier Dulany, was the family patriarch when Harry Worcester Smith arrived. Smith remembered him fondly: "The grand old Colonel, Richard H. Dulany, who led his cavalry regiment at Gettysburg and who in 1853 founded the Upperville Colt and Horse Show, was still the most respected and beloved gentleman in Fauquier and Loudoun counties." The colonel was descended from Daniel Dulany (the Younger), a loyalist, Secretary of the Maryland Colony, an elected member of the Maryland General Assembly, mayor of Annapolis, and author of *Considerations on the Propriety of Imposing Taxes in the British Colonies*, an essay that made such a strong case against taxation without representation that William

Pitt Earl of Chatham used it in his speeches before the British Parliament in favor of repealing the Stamp Act.[2] Daniel married Anna Tasker, daughter of Benjamin Tasker, Provisional Governor of Maryland. Their son Benjamin Tasker Dulany, the colonel's grandfather, was on the right side of the Revolution, loaning General Washington his famous white Arabian "Blueskin" for the duration of the American Revolutionary War. The Dulanys, being Tories, had lost their American fortune after the Revolution, but General Washington introduced Benjamin to Elizabeth French, a wealthy heiress with loads of land in Loudoun County, where their son John Payton Dulany settled with his young wife Mary Ann deButts Dulany.

In 1813, when Mary Ann fell ill, her parents visited her at the home they called Welbourne, a small log cabin on the property. Mary Ann's mother wrote to her family in England about the visit:

"Mr. Dulany's farm is a fine level spot, the land is very rich, has many excellent springs upon it—plenty of wood and stone for building. . . . The house is very small, consisting only of two little rooms below and the same above. Mr. D hopes in a few years by industry and attention to his farm to be enabled to build a more commodious residence. They seem however to be perfectly content & happy in their snug Cottage and if it pleases God . . . they will live comfortably. The neighborhood chiefly consists of plain industrious but independent people, chiefly Quakers, there are very few slaves in that part of Virginia."[3]

John Payton Dulany's farming operation prospered and when the old cabin burned, he moved his family to a larger house on newly acquired land nearby, which the family called Welbourne. John and Mary Ann's son, Richard Henry Dulany, married a rich cousin, Rebecca Ann Dulany, and inherited Welbourne, which grew into a grand four-pillared Neo-Georgian mansion with double matching east and west wings. In 1840 Richard Henry Dulany assembled a pack of foxhounds and established the oldest hunt in America, the Piedmont Foxhounds. He was born a horseman.

Richard Henry had once found a neglected colt, half-frozen, cast against a fence and unable to get up. He took the poor thing home and subsequently resolved to educate his fellow farmers on the importance of careful husbandry of potentially valuable stock, particularly heavy draft crosses so useful to farmers. He and some neighbors formed the Upperville Union Club, which held their first Upperville Horse Show in 1853, the winner of which received a specially designed Tiffany silver cup. Richard Henry Dulany imported two stallions to stand at Welbourne in the hopes of strengthening local stock: "Black Hawk," a Morgan from Vermont, and a four-year-old English-born Cleveland Bay stallion named "Scrivington."

Scrivington was standing at stud at Welbourne when the Civil War broke out, when Grant ordered Sheridan to reduce the Shenandoah Valley, just across the Blue Ridge Mountains from Upperville, to ashes. Though Richard Henry Dulany's family were conservative unionists at heart, he chose to stand by the Virginia Commonwealth's decision to secede, joining Thomas "Stonewall" Jackson's 7th Virginia Cavalry. When his commanding officer, Colonel Turner Ashby, was mortally wounded in 1862, Colonel Richard Henry Dulany took command of the regiment. John Singleton Mosby had formed his infamous guerrilla unit "Mosby's Raiders," stealthily occupying the towns of Aldie, Middleburg, and Upperville along what is now known as the John Mosby Highway—US Route 50.

In answer to Mosby's raids, the Union army, initially polite toward the Dulanys when they came through Welbourne, became more and more belligerent. John Payton Dulany wrote to his son during the war, "I have never in any way taken part in the present war, never in any way approved of secession and did not vote for the secession of the State of Virginia." When the war broke out, Colonel Dulany put his slave-groom, Garner Peters, in charge of Scrivington, sending them both north to Pennsylvania to evade the possibility of either army confiscating the valuable stallion. Peters and Scrivington survived on the stallion's stud fees and returned together to Welbourne when the war ended.

After the war, after the Freedmen's Bureau failed, when deep in the South thousands of former slaves were homeless, destitute, and starving, recovery seemed impossible. Hindsight's lens is terminally fogged. "It is all well enough for us of another generation," W. E. B. Dubois writes in *The*

Souls of Black Folk in 1903, "to wax wise with advice to those who bore the burden in the heat of the day." Even the three post–Civil War amendments to the Constitution could not stop Jim Crow from establishing his ugly nest.

Henry James, the Boston-born novelist living the expat's life in London, traveled through the South early in the twentieth century, hoping to find "the latent poetry of the south," looking for "vivid images, manly, beautiful and sad. I had attached some mystic virtue to the very name Virginia," James writes.[4] He had wanted it to be beautiful; *needed* it to be sentimentally, romantically beautiful. Instead he found a "compromised South," where "the immense grotesque deflated project—extravagant, fantastic and totally pathetic—that had once flourished in Richmond" had revealed its underbelly, where "illiteracy seemed to hover like a queer smell."[5] James was describing Richmond and also Virginia's Tidewater region, where Fort Monroe had once been home to sixty-four thousand displaced slaves in the Grand Contraband Camp. But the whites in Loudoun and Fauquier Counties held themselves apart, politically, from the rest of Virginia.

"Middleburg looked like heaven to me," Erman Downs, an eighty-nine-year-old white man, told historian Eugene Scheel in 1982. "I never saw a place as pretty when I was a youngster."[6] The *Loudoun Mirror* described the area in its historical supplement published in 1909:

"The fields are watered by never-failing streams, in which groves of massive oaks and other valuable timbers grow, affording pastures and comforts for large herds of cattle, fine horses, sheep and swine, and to travel these roads amid the beautiful landscapes and the scenery of majestic Blue Ridge Mountains is surely a pleasure to those who are able to admire the grand and the beautiful."

Though the sidewalks in Middleburg were brick in 1905, the Ashby Gap Turnpike, what is now US Route 50, was a dirt toll road. Animals— pigs and chickens—roamed the streets, but a civic organization was formed in the first decade of the twentieth century to put a stop to that. Middleburg was, and is, a bucolic wayside, as English as an American town can be.[7]

After the Civil War, Loudoun and Fauquier Counties, with their deep rich soils and plentiful water, could afford once again to distance themselves from southern Virginia. Here things were not quite so bad. Though the Bureau of Refugees, Freedmen and Abandoned Lands had not delivered forty acres or a mule to anyone, recovery came more quickly and a strong entrepreneurial spirit among former slaves in Middleburg and Upperville led to the establishment of several nearby villages peopled by former slaves: Marble Quarry, Willisville, Little St. Louis, and Howardsville.[8] The Gaskins of Willisville were closely linked to the Dulanys who, with their deep business interests in New York and Baltimore, did not suffer economic hardships, even after the war. "The Colonel once again farmed the rich and fruitful soil of the Loudoun Valley, the mill was rebuilt, barns were raised . . . he eventually became one of the wealthiest men in the state."[9] The depression of 1893 brought many hardships, but by 1900 the booming agricultural economy in Loudoun and Fauquier Counties helped the region thrive. Successive generations of former slaves became farm and house laborers for newly arriving northerners in search of plentiful, cheap bluegrass land for the thoroughbreds they wanted to raise, race, steeplechase, and hunt. In the fall of 1905, Harry Worcester Smith hired Hamilton Jackson, a well-known Upperville horseman, to be his whipper-in during The Match.

In 1893, in the midst of the worst economic depression the United States had yet experienced, a columnist in the *Loudoun Mirror* may not have understood the historical significance of his observation when he wrote: "A party of sportsmen from New York are expected here this evening to take part in a fox hunt tomorrow."[10] Twelve years later, as the economy recovered, the Northern foxhunters came in earnest. The sheer amount of stuff that the contestants and their friends brought to The Match, and how they got it to Middleburg, boggles the mind. Higginson brought twelve horses, one train-car load, just for himself and his Middlesex staff; the rest of his entourage brought between two and seven horses each, nineteen in all. Smith brought seven horses for himself and his staff; his friends brought eighteen. Additionally, there were a couple of dozen horses stabled around the vicinity for locals and their guests to use. "In all about one hundred crack hunters are stabled here outside of those owned by members of the local hunt."[11] Rooms were rented, meals were taken, extra cooks and scullery maids were needed, grooms were hired, and ladies needed personal maids. Even though Higginson brought "boxes of fruit and many other delicacies that we knew would not be found in the wilds of Virginia," Mrs. Brown, whose rooms he had rented for three weeks, would have had to provide the bulk of his party's needs. "Of course the sleeping accommodations were a bit sketchy," Higginson writes in *Try Back*, his 1931 autobiography, "and the bathing facilities were pretty crude, but we were all there for a lark and everyone was happy—I most of all." Smith's party would have been equally needy, perhaps more so, since Smith was definitely not there for a lark. Even though he and his party stayed at the Dulany's in Upperville, extra servants, cooks, and grooms would have been necessary. How many thousands of dollars went into the local economy as a result of those three weeks? For the Land of the Dulanys, it was only the beginning.

10

Day Four

Saturday, November 4, 1905
Grafton Hunt's Second

"Hounds never ran so fast since the world began."
—Allen Potts, quoting Dr. Charles McEachran, judge
for The Match, *Richmond Times-Dispatch*, Sunday,
November 5, 1905

"You and Ham trot on ahead with the hounds," Smith told Mal Richardson. "We'll not be far behind."

The party from Upperville set off at half-past four from Oakley this fine clear Saturday morning for an hour and a half hack to the meet in Middleburg. Richardson, Hatcher, and Jackson, keeping the coupled hounds within the confines of their triangle, moved off at a good clip, their fresh horses glad to be stretching their legs. They could cover some ground on the Ashby Gap Turnpike, a relatively good road; the visitors from New England were universally appalled at the state of Virginia's roads. Overturned buggies were a common site. Fatal accidents were not infrequent. Smith was inclined to take it a bit slow this morning due to his broken foot.

Neither his fall at Goose Creek nor that stunt with the narrow wooden gate on Friday had slowed Smith down until he had arrived back at Oakley on Friday evening and found that he couldn't get his right boot off. "It doesn't hurt," he'd told Rozier when the latter had noticed him limping toward the house from the stables. Then, when Smith had asked Ham to pull his boot off, it wouldn't budge.

Rozier sent a man down to the village to fetch Dr. Rinker. "And don't bring that new guy Gochnauer, whatever you do," he'd said.

Dr. Rinker had been practicing in the region since the mid-eighties, the man trusted to do everything from set a bone to deliver a baby. He owned the pharmacy next to Piedmont Inn. His buggy drove up at sunset.

Allen Potts, Paul Whitin, Marguerite and Morley Davis, Mal Richardson, and Hal Movius stood around the Dulany sitting room, bourbons in hand, watching the doctor cut Smith's leather boot off with a pair of surgical scissors to inspect his multicolored foot. "You'll have to stay off of it for two weeks," the good doctor told Smith, who laughed in his face—something to which the doctor was not accustomed. "Like it or not," Doc Rinker said, "You'll have to keep it up and stay off of it if you want it to heal."

"I'll hunt if it kills me," Smith said.

"Suit yourself."

"Can't you wrap it?"

"That won't help much."

"I'll keep it up tonight, wrap it in the morning, stick it in a rubber boot and be gone."

"I'll leave a bandage. You appear determined." No one in the room missed the significance of the doctor's understatement.

Next morning, foot wrapped and encased in said rubber boot, Smith was on his way. "You'll have to carry the hounds to the meet, then on to the first covert at the Frank place," he had told Mal Richardson, "but I'll be hunting them as usual." Eight and a half miles to Middleburg, then nearly as far to the meet near the marble quarry at the base of Hog Back Mountain, they would be in the saddle for almost two hours even before hunting began, which is probably why only half the number of people who'd hunted on previous days showed up at Saturday's meet, about twenty-eight in all.

It was still dark as they left Middleburg, so they stayed on roadways and lanes in a circuitous route to Marble Quarry on Goose Creek, home of a plethora of foxes as well as Potomac marble from which the US Capitol's pillars are allegedly built. Sunrise was at 6:13 a.m. Hounds were uncoupled and sent to covert precisely at 6:45. "Sinner," Smith's good cold-line hound, began to whimper almost immediately, but it didn't

Harry Worcester Smith's Bookplate. NATIONAL SPORTING
LIBRARY & MUSEUM ARCHIVES.

Alexander Henry Higginson's Bookplate. ALEXANDER HENRY
HIGGINSON ARCHIVES, NATIONAL SPORTING LIBRARY & MUSEUM.

"Hodo forces the fox to double." Illustration by A. B. Frost for Joel Chandler Harris article on Birdsong's Hodo. *Scribner's Magazine*, 1893. HARRY WORCESTER SMITH ARCHIVES, NATIONAL SPORTING LIBRARY & MUSEUM.

Welbourne, home of Colonel Richard Henry Dulany and site of Opening Meet of The Match. HARRY WORCESTER SMITH ARCHIVES, NATIONAL SPORTING LIBRARY & MUSEUM WITH PERMISSION BY NAT AND SHERRY MORISON.

John Peyton Dulany (1787–1878), father of Colonel Richard Henry Dulany. HARRY WORCESTER SMITH ARCHIVES, NATIONAL SPORTING LIBRARY & MUSEUM WITH PERMISSION BY NAT AND SHERRY MORISON.

Colonel Richard Henry Dulany (1820–1906), 7th Virginia Cavalry. HARRY WORCESTER SMITH ARCHIVES, NATIONAL SPORTING LIBRARY & MUSEUM WITH PERMISSION BY NAT AND SHERRY MORISON.

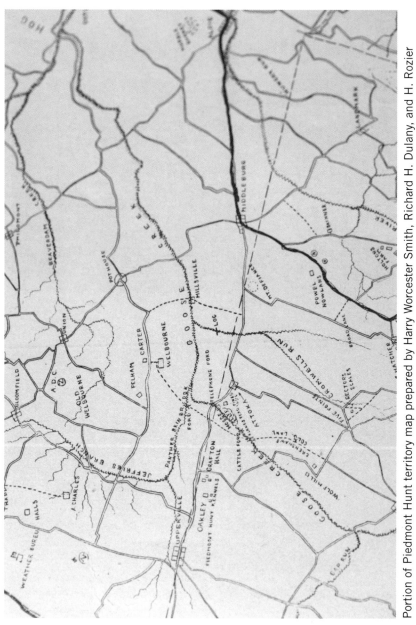

Portion of Piedmont Hunt territory map prepared by Harry Worcester Smith, Richard H. Dulany, and H. Rozier Dulany prior to The Match. WITH PERMISSION BY NAT AND SHERRY MORISON.

Alexander Henry Higginson in full hunt costume: scarlet frock coat, hunting cap, hunting horn, riding crop with thong and lash, black boots with spurs. Middlesex Manor, c.1905. ALEXANDER HENRY HIGGINSON ARCHIVES, NATIONAL SPORTING LIBRARY & MUSEUM.

Alexander Henry Higginson with his son Henry Lee Higginson Jr. and a favorite hound at Middlesex Meadows, c.1905.
ALEXANDER HENRY HIGGINSON ARCHIVES, NATIONAL SPORTING LIBRARY & MUSEUM.

Robert Cotesworth professional huntsman for Middlesex Hounds during The Match with two couple of imported English hounds at Middlesex kennels, Lincoln, MA. ALEXANDER HENRY HIGGINSON ARCHIVES, NATIONAL SPORTING LIBRARY & MUSEUM.

"UPON THE TURF & BENEATH THE TURF ALL MEN ARE EQUAL." Harry Worcester Smith's motto and purple and white racing colors. HARRY WORCESTER SMITH ARCHIVES, NATIONAL SPORTING LIBRARY & MUSEUM.

Artist's depiction of Harry Worcester Smith in Smith's purple and white colors on "The Cad" with handwritten caption by Harry Worcester Smith. HARRY WORCESTER SMITH ARCHIVES, NATIONAL SPORTING LIBRARY & MUSEUM.

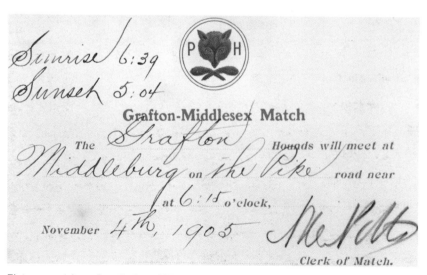

Fixture card from fourth day of The Match signed by Allen Potts, scribe for The Match. ALEXANDER HENRY HIGGINSON ARCHIVES, NATIONAL SPORTING LIBRARY & MUSEUM.

"Old Napper Run, c. 1893." Artist: Arthur Burdett Frost. PRIVATE COLLECTION, MIDLAND, GEORGIA; IMAGE COURTESY NATIONAL SPORTING LIBRARY & MUSEUM.

American Hounds on the run, c.1910. HARRY WORCESTER SMITH ARCHIVES, NATIONAL SPORTING LIBRARY & MUSEUM.

Harry Worcester Smith's ideal American hound, c.1909. HARRY WORCESTER SMITH
ARCHIVES, NATIONAL SPORTING LIBRARY & MUSEUM.

Middlesex Hounds, c.1905, Alexander Henry Higginson, Master, center.
ALEXANDER HENRY HIGGINSON ARCHIVES, NATIONAL SPORTING LIBRARY & MUSEUM.

Robert Cotesworth, Middlesex huntsman, c. 1905, with handwritten caption by Alexander Henry Higginson. ALEXANDER HENRY HIGGINSON ARCHIVES, NATIONAL SPORTING LIBRARY & MUSEUM.

Robert Cotesworth (left) and Alexander Henry Higginson (right) with two imported Middlesex English fox hounds. ALEXANDER HENRY HIGGINSON ARCHIVES, NATIONAL SPORTING LIBRARY & MUSEUM.

Middlesex staff with terrier in a sack on his back, c.1905. ALEXANDER HENRY HIGGINSON ARCHIVES, NATIONAL SPORTING LIBRARY & MUSEUM.

Ladies hunting sidesaddle, c.1905. HARRY WORCESTER SMITH ARCHIVES, NATIONAL SPORTING LIBRARY & MUSEUM.

Marguerite (left) and Westmoreland (right) Davis jumping in tandem, c.1909. "LOUDOUN HUNT, GRAFTON HOUNDS, HARRY WORCESTER SMITH MASTER" PHOTO ALBUM WITH PERMISSION BY DR. JOSEPH AND DONNA ROGERS. PHOTOGRAPHER HERMAN HAAS.

Harry Worcester Smith viewing a fox. "LOUDOUN HUNT, GRAFTON HOUNDS, HARRY WORCESTER SMITH MASTER" PHOTO ALBUM WITH PERMISSION BY DR. JOSEPH AND DONNA ROGERS. PHOTOGRAPHER HERMAN HAAS.

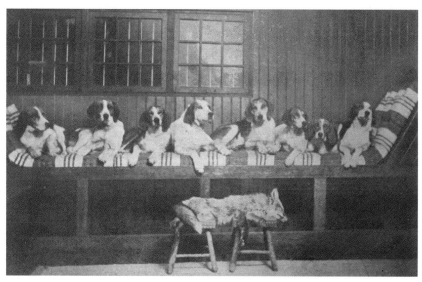

Grafton Hunt Club's American Foxhounds, c.1905. HARRY WORCESTER SMITH ARCHIVES, NATIONAL SPORTING LIBRARY & MUSEUM.

Photograph of Plate (now lost) presented to winner of 1905 Foxhound Match.
HARRY WORCESTER SMITH ARCHIVES, NATIONAL SPORTING LIBRARY & MUSEUM.

Harry Worcester Smith took these men with him to Ireland in 1912. Left to right:
Norman Brooks, Dolph Wheeler, Sam Webster, Wiley Thrash, Joe Thomas. FROM
A Sporting Tour Through Ireland, England, Wales and France BY HARRY WORCESTER
SMITH (COLUMBIA, S.C.: THE STATE COMPANY, 1925.) WITH PERMISSION BY KITTY SMITH.

Harry Worcester Smith c.1940–45, photographer Herman Haas. "LOUDOUN HUNT, GRAFTON HOUNDS, HARRY WORCESTER SMITH MASTER" PHOTO ALBUM WITH PERMISSION BY DR. JOSEPH AND DONNA ROGERS. PHOTOGRAPHER HERMAN HAAS.

A. HENRY HIGGINSON, M. F. H.
Massachusetts

Photo of A. Henry Higginson, president of Master of Foxhound Association, in *The Foxhound Stud Book*, Vol. III, 1910, inscribed "What a crook" and signed H.W.S. by Harry Worcester Smith. WITH PERMISSION BY JOHN GLASS.

amount to much. He and his mates gave that up and continued on down Goose Creek. They didn't strike a true line for more than an hour, but there was nothing slow about their progress. Unlike Higginson and his huntsman Cotesworth, who "picked the hounds up" with their horn periodically to move them from covert to covert or to bring them together if they were separated, Smith let his hounds work at will, trusting them to find and hunt what they could. They spread out far and wide, which was disturbing to those who were used to watching English hounds work. The American hounds' ears dragged the ground, their sterns weren't especially straight, their lack of uniformity in color and look jarred Higginson and his friends. Julian Chamberlain was especially revolted.

"They really do work differently," Allen Potts said to Hal Movius as they watched from a nearby hilltop. Hill-topping is one way to get a broader view of the proceedings. Potts was referring not only to the Grafton and Middlesex hounds, but to their Masters as well.

"It's remarkable," Movius said. He was from Philadelphia and hunted west of Philly with the Brandywine Hunt. "This is rough country, too. I've never seen anything like it."

From their vantage point, they could see all the way to the Potomac and west to the weather station on the eastern slope of the Blue Ridge Mountains. All around them the landscape dipped and swooped toward hundreds of tiny tributaries, then rose again to countless wooded, pastured, and orchard-laden hills.

"I'm used to the flat scrubby land around Henrico County," Potts said. "Considering how hard we've been riding, it's incredible that no one has been more seriously hurt in the past four days. Smith is a maniac."

"You have to admire both men," Movius said judiciously.

Just then the hounds gave tongue and flew along the Goose Creek Valley toward Aldie. Allen Potts saw the fox several hundred yards in front of them. "Tally-Ho!" Potts yelled, standing in his stirrups, doffing his cap in his right hand and using it to point toward the fox. It was a beautiful red fox with a great fat white-tipped brush that shook as it bounded between coverts below them.

"He doesn't seem too worried," Movius said, and the men galloped after the field.

At the first rail fence a man named Duffy came off his horse when it leaped practically from a standstill into the field beyond. Each rider taking his or her own line to jump and follow the hounds resulted in the field spreading out at every fence line, road crossing, or creek crossing and then coming back together on the other side to continue on the hounds' line. It was the hounds' pace that was brutal. As Smith was unable to keep up because of his aching foot, Rozier Dulany attempted to do so, but fell behind when his horse soon became too winded to continue. Other riders tried to do the same. In the end the few who were with hounds after an hour's run had followed those who knew the country well across dozens of short cuts, listening to the hounds in the distance as they ran. Ham Jackson on Smith's pony fell, the victim of a hidden ditch on the other side of a seemingly simple fence. The five-foot drop on the far side, which he didn't notice until mid-air, surprised both him and his pony. They rolled head over heels but came up unscathed.

At the Cross Roads the Grafton hounds lost their scent and checked for about fifteen minutes. Smith had fallen behind. Among the few riders with the hounds was Fred Okie, again acting as Jim Maddux's replacement judge.

"There he goes!" cried another rider, who had chosen to watch from yet another hilltop. The fox could be seen dashing in and out of the underbrush along "the Goose" as the locals called the creek.

"Where's Smith?" someone asked.

"Not here," Hal Movius said.

"In that case," Okie said, "Oui, Sinner, here Sinner," calling Smith's lead hound to him.

"Hey! That's against the rules," Movius yelled. "You can't hunt Smith's pack."

"To hell with the rules," Okie said. "That fox is getting away."

The good hound came running and Okie put him on the track of the viewed fox. Sinner bellowed for his pack mates and off they went again.

Twice the fox swam across Goose Creek; twice the hounds followed. At one crossing Smith and three other riders came off in the mud on the steep slippery creek bank, but they soon remounted and caught up with the pack. When dodging didn't work, the fox took to a straight line across the valley in an effort to outrun the pack. Only nine riders, including Smith, were with the hounds when they came to an abrupt halt at a decrepit tumbledown house on the Pot House road north of Middleburg.

"Sinner! Spic!" Smith called to his lead hounds, trying to cast them in the woods that surrounded the old house. "On to him. Go on," he said. But the hounds kept returning to the house.

"He's got to be under it," Ham Jackson said to Smith as the hounds circled the old foundation again and again. "He must have a hidey-hole under there." Marguerite Davis, the only woman at the end of the run, her husband Morley, Rozier Dulany, the judges Dr. McEachran and Hal Movius, Fred Okie, and Higginson were there.

"Splendid run," Higginson said to Smith, thinking the day was probably over. Horses and riders looked thoroughly spent.

"We're not done yet," Smith said.

"You're kidding," Higginson said.

"Not likely," Smith said ignoring the look of intense disbelief on the faces of those gathered around the old dwelling. "I said I'd hunt until dusk, and I meant it."

"Look here, old man," Dr. McEachran said. "Your hounds have done well."

"You're damn right they have," Smith said.

"Hadn't you better let well enough alone?"

"Well enough isn't good enough. I want a kill."

Rozier Dulany cleared his throat. Smith looked around. He saw in the faces of his friends and rivals a look of elation from the chase mixed with disappointment in his stubborn pride. "Ok. Ok," he said. "Have it your way." In a moment Mal Richardson came trotting up to the house, finally catching up to the Master. "About time," Smith said.

Hal Richardson, Ham Jackson, Rozier Dulany, and Claude Hatcher took the hounds back to Oakley. Higginson and his entourage headed south to Middleburg.

"Are you still thinking of buying that horse?" Julian Chamberlain asked Mrs. Pierce. She had seen a horse that she liked very much belonging to Courtland Smith, Harry's brother, in the Dulany's field.

"I *am* thinking of buying him," Mrs. Pierce said. "I'll drive over this afternoon for another look. I'll need to ride him. There must be a reason he's named Champion."

In the opposite direction, Smith and the Davises walked their horses home to Oakley.

"By God that was a fine run," Westmorland Davis said.

"It was," Marguerite said.

"You've stayed up front every day," Smith said to Marguerite.

"That's thanks to my good string of hunters," she said patting her horse.

"And your riding. No reason for modesty," Smith said.

"Well, someone has to be," she said.

11

For Love, Money, or Marbles

HUNTING IS WARFARE. IT IS SEEK, FIND, BLOOD, AND DEATH. HUNTING IS "the image of war without its guilt."[1] From the Greeks to Tolstoy, when the war horse was the heart of every nation's military-industrial complex, hunting on horseback was recommended as the best preparation for inevitable battles to come. Through hunting "the heroes of antiquity . . . formed themselves for war."[2] Before trucks, tanks, and "aeroplanes," no home, business, or war office was without horses. In music, art, work, and play, horses dominated each day; the strum of hooves beat in every man's ear.

British generals often took a pack of hounds with them on foreign campaigns in order to entertain as well as keep their officers fit. Wellington took a pack with him to Spain during his Peninsular Campaign, which he maintained, "provided excellent sport for the Headquarters Staff."[3] He once jumped a wide hedge lined with Highlanders on his horse "Copenhagen," yelling, "get ready, the French are coming!"[4] In Pretoria during the Second Boer War, Lt. General Edwin Alderson kept a pack, if not of foxhounds, of hunting dogs: "pointers, retrievers, poodles, terriers, Kaffin dogs, and mongrels of all sorts! But they all had hound names, were 'drawn' to feed and exercised like hounds, and they hunted!"[5] When His Majesty's Buckhounds were outlawed in 1900, King Edward VII sent them to South Africa to live their last days hunting jackals with Alderson.[6] In India in 1839, Lord Auckland advanced on Kabul through the Afghan passes with 1000 European troops, 14,000 Indian sepoys, three hundred camels to carry the wine, and a pack of foxhounds.[7] Lt. Colonel John Campbell, V.C. of the Goodstream Guards and MFH for seventeen years of the Tanat Side Harriers, earned the Victorian Cross at the First Battle of Somme, in which he rallied his men with a hunting horn.[8] The Royal Harithyah Hunt Committee of Baghdad published *Riding to Hounds* (printed by the Iraq Army Press) as late as 1953 to remind members of etiquette when chasing the jackal: "for the most part represent the general procedure in England with such amendments as are required for Iraqi conditions." Captain Lionel Dawson of the Royal Navy expresses what many felt up to and even after the Great War when he writes, "surely we are not claiming too much in saying that no other Army [than the British] in the World could have produced more gallant and confident leadership; nor could the comradeship of sport in war have been so gloriously exemplified."[9]

On our side of the Atlantic, Theodore Roosevelt carried the banner of manliness in a crusade against pansy pacifists. "We do not admire the man of timid peace," he proclaimed in his "Strenuous Life" speech to Chicago businessmen in 1899. "We admire the man who embodies victorious effort." He admired the British Empire for "advancing the cause of civilization" and urged his countrymen to "play our part well in the great work of uplifting mankind." Teddy extolled the manly sports as a preparation for war; he hunted regularly with the Meadowbrook Hunt, a drag-hunt on Long Island. In his little tome for boys, "American Boy," published in *St. Nicholas* in May of 1900, he tells his readers that "the chief serious use of fox-hunting is to encourage manliness and vigor, and to keep men hardy." Roosevelt recognized that the South was better prepared at the beginning of the Civil War chiefly because of their ability to ride to hounds.[10] "If, in 1860," Roosevelt writes in *The Century Magazine* (July 1886) "riding to hounds had been in the North, as it was in the South, a national pastime, it would not have taken us until well on towards the middle of the war before we were able to develop a cavalry capable of withstanding the shock of Southern horsemen."

Oliver Wendell Holmes Jr. remembered his years fighting for the Twentieth Massachusetts in the Civil War in his famous Memorial Day 1895 speech to Harvard's graduating class. "We still believe," he proclaimed, "that the joy of life is living, is to put out all one's powers as far as they will go; that the measure of power is obstacles overcome; to ride boldly at what is in front of you, be it fence or enemy; to pray, not for comfort, but for combat. . . . If once in a while in our rough riding a neck is broken, I regard it, not as a waste, but as a price well paid for the breeding of a race fit for headship and command."

Theodore Roosevelt must have had this in mind when he formed the First US Cavalry in the Spanish American War. Made up of riding men, mainly from the Southwest, the Rough Riders prepared for their war as a standard cavalry unit. However, they had to leave most of their horses and half their men back in Tampa when they embarked for the Philippines since a quarter of the men had already succumbed to malaria or yellow fever. His men were forced to run up the San Juan Hill on foot. Nevertheless, Teddy, astride "Texas," waved his hat and yelled a cavalry charge.

Nineteenth- and early-twentieth-century literature is another repository for praise of foxhunting as excellent preparation and execution of warfare. Lev Nikolayevich (Leo) Tolstoy, whose family were members of Russia's nineteenth-century aristocracy, writes with familiarity about hunting and war. His fictional hero, the young Count Rostov who loved to hunt fox and wolf with his borzoi hounds, watched the Battle of Borodino "with his keen sportsman's eye . . . [he] gazed at what was happening before him as at a hunt . . . he acted as he did when hunting."[11]

Siegfried Sassoon, a member of England's last generation to fight on horseback and author of the beautiful and nearly forgotten World War I *Memoirs of a Foxhunting Man*, wrote with eloquence, nostalgia, and sharp poignancy of his naïvety before the war. Born to a wealthy merchant family in Kent, Sassoon (a pseudonym) writes about learning to ride behind his Aunt Evelyn's groom, Dixon, on a pony named "Rob." Dixon had aspirations of being a sporting man's groom and convinced Sassoon's aunt to buy a succession of good mounts to fulfill his, if not the boy's, dreams. But the boy came around when he found friendship on the hunt field. He bought his splendid hunter, "Cockburn," for £50 from under a "moody-faced youth" who knew not what he'd owned. A "handsome bay horse, nothing flashy, fine limbs, sloping shoulders and deep chest," Cockburn stood on the hunt field "as quiet as if he were having his picture painted."[12] Cockburn taught Sassoon what it meant to have a hunter who could keep up with the best. Before the war Sassoon moved with Cockburn to Peterborough for a season to ride and hunt alongside his friend Dennis Milden (a fictional name for Norman Loder) with the Ringwell (Southdown) Hunt. "My heart quickened," he writes about hunting and jumping Cockburn, "at the way my horse took [the jumps], shortening and then quickening his stride and slipping over them with an ease and neatness which were a revelation to me."

Sassoon writes in retrospect, in 1923, with an intense nostalgia, a sense of what was lost and how little gained before and after the world was aware that a war could encompass the globe. "It was to my advantage," he writes when the war came, "that I was already known to Colonel Winchell as a hunting man. For I always found that it was a distinct asset, when in close contact with officers of the Regular Army, to be able to converse convincingly about hunting. It gave me almost an unfair advantage in some ways." Near the end of the third book in the trilogy, *Sherston's Progress*, after long ago relinquishing Cockburn to an officer in hopes of saving him from the infantry lines, he finds himself back at the front in France, hacking twenty miles at dawn on "a quadruped who has left me no describable memory, except that he suffered from string-halt and his hind-leg action was the only lively thing about him." He'd survived in no small part *because* he was a hunting man. "I was trotting past the shuttered houses of some un-awakened village, with the sun just coming up beyond the roadside poplars. What I felt was a sort of personal manifest of being intensely alive . . . not because of the War, but in spite of it."[13]

⁕

January of 1905 came to New England dressed as a lamb. Though a wet snow had fallen on New Year's Day, it was gone in a week and within a fortnight the Middlesex and Grafton hunts were able to resume hunting. Years later, Alexander Henry Higginson would write in his memoir, *Try Back*, that Harry Worcester Smith "rather antagonized me," that winter, confessing "I was somewhat amazed at my temerity in taking on my shoulders the defense of the English foxhound."[14] As late spring came in like a lion, with over twenty-one inches of snow that March, Higginson's and Smith's letters to *Rider and Driver* took a warlike tone. Unable to limit his focus to hound dogs, Smith's rhetoric became laced with patriotic zeal. "Is it any wonder that in the turmoil of the last one hundred years more time and thought should have been put into the breeding of young Americans of a type that would be successful, than of breeding foxhounds of a type?" Higginson, for his part, refused to engage: "I do not care to go into a long personal argument with Mr. Smith regarding the merits of things English and American, which have, to my mind, little or nothing to do with the question which we are discussing." But Smith kept it up and enlarged his scope: "we have just enough pride in America," he writes, "to be willing to back the Grafton Hunt with American hounds, American thorough-bred horses with saddles and bridles . . . the best that can be made in the United States of America; the livery made in American mills by American operatives, from the tip of the boot to the velvet on the cap, against the imported production." Smith clearly considered Higginson a "daddy's boy" with nothing to do but ride and hunt and travel to England to buy hounds. Smith writes, "Unfortunately, I am obliged to work as well as play." It must have struck some readers as absurd, while ringing true with others when Smith upped the ante another notch that February: "in this great and glorious United States of America we have men who do things; and are not tied down and held back by theory, codes of rules, manners, and customs of a nation whose geographical position, temperature, make-up of soil, and make-up of men, are entirely different from ours."

Enough!

"I suggest that we bind the matter," Smith writes in March, "by depositing $250 each in the hands of the editor of *Rider and Driver* July 1st, the same amount August 1st, the same amount September 1st, the same amount October 1st, the same to stand as a forfeit should either pack or master at any time after July 1st decide to withdraw from the trial." Higginson complies: "So far as I am concerned, I should be best pleased if the match might take place in Virginia in the Piedmont Valley."

Having no battlefield on which to show their skills as hunting men, they made their own.

12

Day Five

Monday, November 6, 1905
Middlesex Hunt's Third

"It may be said with exact truth that the whole Valley is taking the liveliest interest in this great sporting event, which is without doubt the most remarkable trial of hounds from every standpoint that has ever taken place."
—ALLEN POTTS, *RICHMOND TIMES DISPATCH*, TUESDAY, NOVEMBER 7, 1905

"YOU RECKON HE'S UNDER THERE?" JIM MADDUX ASKED ROBERT Cotesworth, pointing to a giant boulder in the woods near Fry's Dam on Goose Creek.

Cotesworth just nodded and continued to congratulate his hounds. "Well done, my bonnies," he crooned to them, and one by one they came to lick the hand that fed them.

"You holed your fox," Maddux quizzed the huntsman further. "Why don't you put your terriers to work?" Each of the Middlesex whips rode with a little fox terrier in a pouch on his back. Just now they were both yapping to get down.

Cotesworth looked at the boulder, then at the judge and said, "It's not terriers you want sir, but a big stick of dynamite to do the trick."

"Ha!" Maddux said, slapping the little huntsman on his back. "Well said, my friend." Maddux had not been up with the first flight of riders, who had followed the hounds to their fox's den. He had taken a bad fall when his thoroughbred mare named "Firefly" ran into a hidden double

97

strand of wire over a stone fence earlier in the morning. Maddux was bruised badly but otherwise fine; his mare's shoulder was cut deeply and he had her sent home with a groom. She would probably be unable to hunt for some time. Maddux had subsequently hitched a ride in a buggy with some spectators, locals who knew their way around, and followed the hunt along the many byways and farm lanes in the neighborhood.

"What a run that was," Emily Ladenburg said to her friend Leonard Ahl as they circled their tired horses near the fox's den. They were both in the Higginson camp and very happy to have seen the English hounds make such a fine showing on this, the fifth day of The Match. The night before, Sunday, there had seen a rainstorm with high winds. The rain had stopped in the early hours and the added moisture had made hunting conditions just about perfect. The hills and creeks thereabouts guaranteed that the land drained quickly, making it unlikely that the horses would run into deep mud to slow their progress and though the creeks ran high this morning, there were plenty of good fords to cross if you knew your way around. Mind you, there were plenty of ditches now full of water and the stream banks were slippery. Mr. Ahl had brought a string of horses from Long Island and Mrs. Ladenburg, a widow and expert rider also from Long Island, was riding one of his.

"Beautiful," Mr. Ahl said. "You could have put a blanket over the pack, it was running so tight."

"The fox seemed to have had as much fun as we did," Mrs. Ladenburg said.

"I know. At one point I saw him lollygagging down the valley like it was a day in the park. He took them on a goose chase and circled back just as easy as you please."

"I must say," Jim Maddux said to Higginson. "You've proven me wrong."

"How's that?" Higginson asked.

"I've said all along that English hounds are too heavy, too clumsy, too much bone and weight to chase our foxes here in Virginia."

"Oh?"

"I didn't believe English hounds could run so fast."

"I'm glad you've seen the light, Mr. Maddux," Higginson said.

"However, I still don't think there could have been a kill today," Maddux continued. "They certainly ran well, but I don't believe they were fast enough to catch and kill the fox."

"Oh pooh," Mrs. Ladenburg said. "You don't have to be such a spoilsport."

———

Sunday had been a day of rest and, coincidentally, Harry Worcester Smith's forty-first birthday. There had been a party at Oakley, a luncheon for thirty-eight guests. More Virginians from farther south and across the Blue Ridge Mountains, including Mr. Ed Butler from Clarke County, had traveled to Upperville for the second week of hunting. There was not a country inn or hospitable home for a radius of twenty miles that did not welcome riders and their horses for the event, and they all gathered at Oakley to rehash The Match on Sunday, November 5, 1905. A sumptuous meal was held in the Dulany dining room. Virginia ham and turkey, vegetables from the root cellar and canned from the garden, even some late chard and greens that had not yet been frostbitten, and beaten biscuits, a specialty of the house, was accompanied by plenty of French wine, champagne, and Kentucky bourbon. All around the gigantic table discussions were held involving crashes, mash-ups, calamities, and close calls.

Every day thus far horses and riders had traveled great distances; just the day before, Saturday, it was estimated that the riders had traveled a full fifty miles including hacking to the meet, following hounds, and returning home to Middleburg or Upperville. There had been between three and seven falls every day. Some horses were injured badly enough to prevent them hunting for the remainder of The Match and some for the remainder of the season, which lasted through March in Virginia. Though Higginson's broken ribs and Smith's broken foot were the worst injuries so far, there were plenty of bruises at the party, hidden beneath elegant clothing, and there were still eight more days of hunting in the coming week and a half.

"It's nothing short of miraculous that no one has been more seriously hurt," Allen Potts had said.

"That's easy for you to say, Potts," Smith had said, raising his plaster-casted foot above the table. Doctor Rinker had returned on Sunday morning after church to apply a cast that would fit into Smith's boot. Smith's chair was at one end of the table, where he propped his foot on a stool. His brother, Courtland, sat next to him. Courtland had not been able to hunt thus far due to a broken collarbone he'd acquired over a practice jump the day before The Match began. Rozier Dulany had missed the first two days of The Match due to a sprained wrist he'd gotten the same day in the same way.

Smith proposed the first toast: "To the Master of Middlesex and his guests." Everyone stood to drink to Higginson, who in turn proposed: "To the Piedmont of Virginia, the finest hunting country I've ever seen—the Market Harborough of America." Glasses rang.

"To Colonel Richard Henry Dulany, the greatest horseman and most gracious host a country could boast," Smith said.

"To Harry Worcester Smith," Rozier Dulany said, bringing out an ancient pair of wooden crutches. "Happy Birthday, old man."

Monday, November 6, the fifth day of The Match and Middlesex Hound's third, had begun at 7:00 a.m. on Main Street in Middleburg, where the whole village had turned out to see the English pack set out for the day's hunting. By this time Higginson and his crowd had secured quite a following in the village. Before setting off, he and Mrs. Brown offered coffee to the riders and anyone else who wanted a hot beverage on this damp morning. A few followers passed a flask with which to fortify the coffee. It felt to Higginson like an important day, a day when his hounds could show excellent sport *and* kill a fox. Up to this point both packs had drawn blank days, both had had a good day with a fox brought to ground, but neither had had a kill.

The first cast was in the woods at the base of Bald Hill on the Fred farm north of Middleburg toward Pot House. Shortly there came a cry from Visitor and a couple of his friends. Cotesworth got the message and blew his horn for the rest of the pack to join him.

"There's the difference, right there," Smith said to Rozier Dulany as they took off after the pack down the Goose Creek valley once again. "He has to pick them up and point them in the right goddam direction. My Spic would have found, given tongue, rounded up the pack on his own, and we would have been on our way three minutes ago. *That's* why they'll never kill a fox in Virginia!"

Just then Mrs. Pierce galloped past and yelled, "We'll see about that!"

The fox, viewed by Mr. Fred himself, the owner of the farm, circled Bald Hill and took flight, probably toward his home territory down "the Goose." The field of riders had swelled and there were some new-comers out this morning. One, a Mr. Belt, landed in a slippery ditch on the other side of a wall, fell off and was unable to continue the rest of the day. Another, Dick Lawson—a member of the Piedmont Hunt—also fell after yet another wall, but he was able to remount and join the fun.

Allen Potts stationed himself on a hilltop where he got a good view of the whole affair. "That fox was just playing with those hounds," he told Rozier Dulany later. "I watched him run across two fields, run along the wall, jump down and backtrack in his own footsteps then take off for the Smith farm. Then I viewed him again on the Duffy place where he ran into that drove of cattle to throw them off."

The herd of cattle had caused the hounds to check, to lose their quarry, for about five minutes. Good old Visitor found the new line and went away again, Cotesworth blowing the welcome "Gone Away" tune for the second time that morning. For nearly an hour the crafty critter led the hounds on a vulpine adventure, jumping onto and running along rail fences, across more walls, down the creek, and out again before coming back to what was undoubtedly his own den under the boulder in the woods, just three minutes in front of the hounds.

"Those were the three minutes I was talking about," Smith said to Rozier Dulany as they stood round the boulder watching Cotesworth congratulate his hounds.

"Your hounds could have caught him?" Rozier asked. "That was a pretty spectacular run."

"These English hounds are not fast enough. They can't scale these walls and fences like my hounds can. They're good, but they're not good enough." Smith, as always, was not keeping his pronouncements quiet.

He had a loud voice for such a little man with only one lung. Or maybe it was just his opinions that were loud.

"He's just a loudmouth braggart," Julian Chamberlain told his friend Higginson, noticing that Higginson was taking Smith's comments to heart. "That was a fine run. Don't forget that."

"Yes," Higginson said. "But it wasn't a kill."

13

Evolution!

"It is an awkward word to deal with in a chapter."[1]

WHO KNEW? CHARLES DARWIN WAS A FOXHUNTER! HIS FATHER WARNED
that he would come to nothing, disgrace himself and his family, that all he
cared for was "shooting, dogs and rat-catching,"[2] but he and his appropriately named cousin William Fox, with their gun dogs Sappho, Fan, and
Dash, spent their vacations from Oxford hunting birds and foxes in Der-
byshire, where William's family leased the four-thousand-acre Osmaston
Hall. Charles had grown up around dogs and loved them until his dying
day. His terrier Polly died just days after her master, in April of 1882.
Dogs played an important part in Charles Darwin's careful reasoning *On
the Origin of Species Through Natural Selection* (1858).

Evolution has become synonymous with change. But unless you
introduce time, great unimaginable stretches of time, the changing of a
breed is not evolution. Even considering the one or two hundred years
of careful breeding, a paltry scant epoch when compared with the eons
required for a species to evolve, the foxhound has not so much evolved as
changed at the hands of its breeders in response not only to conditions,
but to fads. Though the English and American foxhound has changed
again and again, to say that it has *evolved* is a misnomer.

Charles Darwin recognized the importance of time in evolution's
equation when he compared his observations taken over his five-year
voyage, beginning in December of 1831, aboard the *Beagle* to those he
recorded when consulting England's best hound, cattle, and bird breeders on his return. He sought and found friendships with men like Hugh
Dalziel, greyhound breeder and author of *British Dogs; Their History,*

Characteristics, Breeding and Management and the famous naturalist William Yarrell, author of *A History of British Birds*, who convinced Darwin to keep and breed "fancy" pigeons. Darwin devised his theory of evolution through natural selection aboard and after the *Beagle*'s voyage concurrently and by contrast with his observations of unnatural or "artificial" selection in domestic breeds, specifically cattle, pigeons, pheasants, and hounds. "Natural selection," he writes, "is a power incessantly ready for action, and is as immeasurably superior to man's feeble efforts, as the works of nature are to those of art. . . . Nature gives successive variations; man adds them up in certain directions useful to him."

What we're really talking about when we talk about breeding, about artificial selection, is genetics, and Darwin didn't know much about genetics. Though Gregor Mendel had published his paper on peas in 1866, Darwin had not read it, nor did Mendel's findings on inheritance become a part of the new evolutionary lexicon until his work was rediscovered early in the twentieth century. The science of genetics, of inheritance through the transfer of DNA, was not established until late in the 1920s.

Even when bolstered by science, with the knowledge of dominant and recessive traits, hound breeders can only go so far in predicting a pup's potential. There are too many variables, too much subjective preference, to pin the outcome on science. Floppy ears, color, curly hair, curly stern; those are the predictable things, but a really great instinct, intelligence, what's called "keenness" is much harder to predict. "Man can rarely select, or at least only with much difficulty, any deviation of structure excepting of such as is externally visible," Darwin writes. Only recently, in 2010, geneticists proved indisputably through a study of mitochondrial DNA that every dog on earth is descended from one ancient ancestor: the Middle Eastern gray wolf.[3] What hound breeders are really looking for then—in a docile, trainable dog with a good nose, eager to hunt and kill—is an immature wolf.

Frank Townend Barton, author of *Hounds*, writes with not a little arrogance about what foxhound breeders believed they could produce at the end of the nineteenth century: "The Foxhound is built upon lines displaying greater economy of material than that of any other dog. . . . Every ounce of bone and muscle is placed where it can be utilized to the best advantage . . . every inch of its anatomy being specifically developed to obtain the maximum result compatible with purpose of design." Habit, that is, knowledge acquired by repetition throughout a hound's life, is not transferable. Instinct and intelligence would be the most desirable, and hardest, traits to select for. The early nineteenth century was the age of phrenology, when the size and shape of a person's (and a dog's) head supposedly gave a glimpse of his innate intelligence. Hound breeders in England wanted big square heads, "knowledge boxes," to better carry a big brain and presumably more smarts, more innate instinct to find, follow, and catch a fox. Knightley William Horlock, author of *The Science of Foxhunting*, writes in 1868, "For choice, we would select a square head in preference to an oblong one, because we have, through extensive experience, seen the greatest amount of sagacity in the canine species exhibited by such knowledge boxes." Horlock's friend John Ward at least had a sense of humor about it: "Our hounds possess rather large knowledge boxes, but there is this advantage connected with them: their heads are so heavy, that when once their noses reach the ground, they manifest great reluctance in raising them again."[4]

In 1837 there were fewer than twenty recognized breeds of dogs; by 1850 there were forty; in 1859 England held her first organized dog show; in 1873 the Kennel Club was founded; the Peterborough Hound Show in 1888; and in 1891 there were over two thousand dogs in Cruft's Greatest Dog Show, the first at which all breeds were invited to the Royal Agricultural Hall in Islington. Dog breeding was a Victorian craze, the idea being to establish and "purify" the breeds. Fads had begun to dictate breeds; foxhounds, in neither England nor America, were above the fray.

A succession of events—of changing country, horses, riding style, social norms, and aesthetics—brought about changes in foxhunting sport in England in the mid- to late-nineteenth century. It's a chicken-or-egg argument, a question of which brought about what, surrounding changes in preferred types of hounds and horses and even the fox they chased. Barton writes: "If we attempted to touch upon the evolution of hounds we should also have to renew the whole evolution of social life and sport, for the one has influenced the other, and the twain have combined to bring about the evolution [there's that word again] of manners, customs, life generally and the horse and hound essentially."

England's eighteenth- and nineteenth-century Inclosure Acts took foxhunting from a slow all-day-and-into-the-night affair across open "clean" fields where the work of a methodical pack was appreciated and encouraged by men and women on cobs and farm horses, to a three- or four-hour game on fast thoroughbreds that could jump timber and banks enclosing the pastures. Riders had to be back to the city to work by afternoon. Adrenaline became the drug of choice and people began to turn out as much if not more to ride than to watch hounds work. In response, men like Hugo Meynell began to breed faster hounds lest the poor dogs be run over, jumped on, and killed. "Using the latest techniques of in-and-in breeding developed by Robert Bakewell (Charles Darwin's friend) with his New Leicester sheep, Meynell bred a pack capable of keeping up with a fast-running fox at midday."[5]

This was "the golden era of foxhound breeding from 1780–1873, in which British sportsmen lay awake nights thinking about hound specifications . . . hound impresarios such as Meynell, Osbaldeston, Musters, Barry, Corbet, Drake, Warde, Sutton, Beaufort, Middleton, Fitzwilliam, Bentinck and others became famous in and out of [British] kennels."[6] Lord Henry Bentinck bred for working qualities like stamina and wind, and he wrote a little book called *Goodall's Practice* about the great huntsman William Goodall's techniques for training foxhounds. Goodall had good advice for hound-men and husbands: "Hounds should be treated like women; that they would not bear to be bullied, to be deceived, or neglected with impunity."[7] Goodall was a professional huntsman for the Duke of Rutland's Belvoir Hounds 1841–1859. "Toward the mid-nineteenth century, that celebrated hound-man, Lord Henry Bentinck, was breeding a pack second to none; lightly built, active sorts which possessed iron constitutions and could endure the hardest days."[8]

"Breeders habitually speak of an animal's organization," Darwin writes in *Origin*, "as something plastic, which they can mold almost as they please." The Victorians had an appetite for collection and they were practically obsessed with natural curiosities. Coupled with worldwide British colonialism and simultaneous awakenings in science and industrial technology, it's no wonder they could and did play God with their domestic breeds.

Late in the nineteenth century change came again to the English foxhound. In the mid-1800s England had four distinct types of foxhounds: the square-headed Badminton hounds of Beaufort; the Belvoir hounds, rather fine with short heads; Welsh rough-coated hounds, and the Fitzwilliam with elegant long heads. By 1900 there was a push to unify the look. Dog shows and hound shows pressured for a "type" and the "Peterborough" hound became popular. He was a big, broad-chested, heavy-boned hound standing twenty-six inches with eight-inch forearms and weighing as much as eighty pounds. Bred for the fashionable Peterborough Hound Show, he had to be "plumb straight" to win. He was perfected in a short period of intense in-breeding between the late 1800s and the First World War. It doesn't take long to alter a breed—about one man's lifetime in fact. Though he was writing about cattle and sheep breeders, Darwin could have been writing about hound breeders when he writes: "It is certain that several of our eminent breeders have, even within a single lifetime, modified to a large extent their breeds."[9]

Those who did not admire the new type of foxhound called them "Shorthorn" for their resemblance to English shorthorn cattle, or "Peterborough" because the Peterborough Hound Show is often blamed for promoting "an obsession with breeding for looks."[10] The Belvoir (pronounced beaver) kennels were best known for this type, producing look-alike "Belvoir tan" hounds, a rich red with a white necktie. Packs of "Belvoiry" hounds looked like monocultures of clones. They were not without their advocates, however. Frank Gillard, the Belvoir huntsman from 1860 to 1896, is credited by some for "elevating the pack to the distinction of being the best in the world."[11] Belvoir's "Gambler's" skeleton was set up "as a model of symmetry and proportion to illustrate a perfect hound."[12]

When Alexander Henry Higginson traveled to England in 1900 to find and purchase a pack of English foxhounds, he entered the British hound-breeding controversy. It was from one of the fashionable Peterborough-winning packs, the Fitzwilliam, that Higginson purchased his first drafts of English hounds. "I was only [in England] for about six weeks, and I met among others two men who were to have a great deal of influence on my hunting career . . . George C. W. Fitzwilliam, Master of the Fitzwilliam (Milton) pack and Charles Isaac huntsman at the time for Mr. Fernie."[13] Higginson visited Mr. Fernie's pack for a look at the hounds. After a glass of port and some hound talk, Isaac took him to the kennels. Higginson writes in his memoir *Try Back*, "little as I knew about hounds, I did know in a minute that they were a very useful lot."[14] Of Fitzwilliam, Higginson writes, "though I did not have a chance at that time to go down to his kennels at Peterborough I had many talks with him, and after my return to America he sent me a stallion hound called Visitor that helped a lot in my breeding operations."[15] Just before The Match Higginson described Visitor, a hound he bought from Mr. Fernie's pack who was bred in 1899, in an op-ed in *Rider and Driver*: "he was by Milton Redcar (1890) out of Belvoir Vigilana, 1895, and is a big, upstanding sort with the best of feet and legs and great substance, a quality so essential to prevent the tendency of thoroughbred English hounds to deteriorate in bone after a few generations in America. . . . The weedy, chance-bred 'American hound,' so called, exemplifies this tendency."

Was Higginson, knowingly or otherwise, bowing to the Peterborough fashion? During The Match, the *Boston Herald* reported that Mr. Higginson's pack "was remarkably handsome, the markings all being practically the same, so much so, it is said, that no one except Mr. Higginson and Cotesworth [his huntsman] are able to distinguish one from the other." But problems came with the new type; straightness made for short pasterns and cat feet, ending in conformation flaws such as turned-out elbows, knuckled-over knees, pigeon toes, and footpad problems. Keep in mind that these hounds were required to run up to fifty miles a day, six days a week from October to March. Eight years—five working seasons—is as long as one can expect a working foxhound to live. The Belvoir hound could not have been more different from his American counterpart.

~~~

Perhaps apropos to the Brits' conception of America in general, the history of at least one strain of the nineteenth-century American foxhound began with stolen property. Tom Harriss, a traveling stock man, was on his way back to Kentucky through the Cumberland Mountains in

Tennessee sometime in the early 1850s when he heard a pack of hounds running. What possessed him to jump the lead hound and steal him, other than to make a buck when he got home, is anybody's guess. At any rate, the hound, who became known as "Tennessee Lead," was sold to George Washington Maupin, the son of a Virginia transplant living in Madison County, Kentucky. When, soon afterward, the red fox crossed the Appalachian Mountains and invaded the grey's Kentucky territory, Tennessee Lead was the only hound in Maupin's pack who knew how to chase it. Maupin's partner was John W. Walker; his grandson, writing in 1945, described Tennessee Lead as a "medium-sized black dog, with thin hair, a small tan spot over each eye and no brush on his tail. He had a clear short mouth, plenty of fox sense, plenty of speed—in fact he had all the qualifications necessary for a high class dead game foxhound."[16] In search of more like him, Maupin sent his sons back to Tennessee to acquire a few, but what came back proved the rule of inheritance: "what they got did resemble him in looks, but there the resemblance ended."[17] Hoping to pass Lead's knowledge of the red fox to his offspring, "every hunter who could, raised a litter of pups from him."[18] Woods Walker's book on his family's foxhound breeding operation reads like the book of Genesis: "Gooch's Ida II was by Dolph out of Trim II. Dolph is by Imported Bragg out of Flourence. Trim II is by Spotted Top out of Ida, she by Tennessee Lead out of Trim . . ."

From the middle of the nineteenth century on, from northeast to southwest along the Eastern Seaboard in the Appalachian Mountains, American foxhounds were asked to hunt a wilder red fox through scrubby bush on steep slopes along narrow ridges. Whereas the native grey fox would confine himself to a small area around his den, circling, darting, zigzagging like a rabbit, and then as soon as not, climbing a tree like a cat to escape a pack of hounds, southern sportsmen soon found out that their hounds, bred to run the circling grey, were no match for a long, straight-running red who brought his reputation with him as he advanced down the Appalachian chain. "The hunters found that they wanted dogs with speed, grit, bottom, and noses more keenly alive to the situation."[19] The men who bred them—the Maupins, the Walker brothers of Tennessee, the Triggs of Kentucky, Dr. Henry of Virginia, and Mr. Birdsong of Georgia, "constantly strove to produce a hound that could start, track and drive a red fox, with few faults, from day-light to dark, any day and every day."[20]

Whereas English studbooks on foxhound breeding went as far back as the early eighteenth century, record keeping for American foxhounds was Spartan if anything. When Harry Worcester Smith decided to quit steeplechasing and take up foxhunting, he went to Virginia to build his pack. He had been hunting regularly in upstate New York with Colonel Wadsworth's hounds, "watching English hounds trying to follow the American red fox in the Genesee Valley."[21] In the fall of 1896, Thomas Hitchcock brought a pack of American hounds to the Genesee, impressing Smith, "but it was not until 1898 that I had a chance of seeing a pack of Virginia fox-killing hounds."[22] As the guest of H. Rozier Dulany, who would sponsor The Match six years later, Smith got a taste of the country he came to love and the hounds he spent the rest of his life promoting. He chose hounds from Burr Frank Bywaters's pack, and from Charles Bunning's Cold Springs, Kentucky, pack for his primary stock. Within three seasons he had purchased over 150 hounds and he sent this three best, Simple, Sinner, and Spic to Virginia to test their mettle with Bywaters's pack. Bywaters declared them no better but no worse than his own hounds and he and Smith became partners in breeding American foxhounds.

Smith was looking for and breeding for—no less intensely than the Peterborough men—a type, a color, a look, which he began to call "Grafton markings." He bred for a "black saddle, white ring about the neck, white legs, one-half white tail, white strip in face, tan head—the identical markings as the Belvoir hound."[23] How could he have bred for the "identical markings as the Belvoir hound?" Because, although his sources, Bywaters and Bunning, declared that there was no English blood in their packs, Harry W. Smith knew that English and Irish blood was original to all American foxhounds, especially Virginia hounds.

Alexander Mackay-Smith, the undisputed expert on American foxhounds, author of *The American Foxhound 1747–1967*, admits that American "Foxhunters are notoriously lazy about keeping records."[24] Thomas, 6th Lord Fairfax, imported a pack of hounds to his Virginia home in what is now the Blue Ridge Hunt territory sometime in the mid-eighteenth century. If the men from whom Smith acquired his stock had kept record, they would most probably have pinpointed their origins, not only to Lord Fairfax's hounds, but also to "Mountain" and "Muse," the dog and bitch imported to the Baltimore area about 1814 by an Irishman named Bolton Jackson. Mountain and his get in Maryland became the foundation stock for the Birdsong and Henry packs in Georgia and Virginia, while Tennessee Lead and his get became the Kentucky and Tennessee foundation stock. When the Lead hounds became too inbred, two more English hounds were imported to shore up the breed: "Marth" and "Rifler," a bitch and dog imported by one of the Walkers through a English merchandiser, William Fleming, who also loved to foxhunt and spent his vacations with the Walkers and Maupins in Kentucky. Marth and Rifler came from the Scottish Duke of Buccleuch's pack, established in 1827, the foundation of which is "Belvoir Singwell" (1864), who would have been bred by William Goodall, huntsman for Belvoir from 1843 to 1869. Woods Walker writes that the two hounds were shipped by boat to New York, by rail to Cincinnati, and then by stagecoach to Richmond, Kentucky, "and when they arrived nearly all the hunters were there to meet them."[25]

Burrell Frank Bywaters admittedly "paid little attention to pedigrees or registrations."[26] Though Smith said emphatically that he cared not what a hound looked like, as long as it could chase down and kill a red fox, he also knew that, in order to achieve his goal of establishing a recognized breed, the *American* foxhound, he would have to transform the theretofore haphazard breeding methods of his countrymen to a standardized, record-keeping, uniform lot. When it came to his hounds' color, he was ruthless: "those not properly marked are killed at birth."[27] When it came to size, he chose small—"20 to 21½—for up-hill, down-dale, day in and day out work."[28]

Smith and his fellow breeders, Bywaters and Bunning, were most specific about a hound's voice. Bywaters liked to say, "I like a hound with a good drawing musical tongue that will almost make the hair stand on your head."[29] Why voice? Because, unlike English hounds who hunted over open moist country with plenty of scent, the American breeders knew that their American hounds had to practically hunt by themselves, to spread out and look carefully for a cold scent sometimes eight hours old, and when (not *if*, but *when*) then found, they had to sing out, to gather their pack members, and chase the red as one. The men who followed must hope only to keep up. Since they wouldn't be able to follow closely through thicket and bramble, they had to be able to hear their hounds and anticipate their trail, in hopes of being at the end for the kill.

And the last thing Smith, Bywaters, and Bunning were breeding for was the American foxhound that could and would run in a pack. The Triggs and Walkers had been breeding field-trial hounds who hunted, possibly in twos and threes, but mainly as individuals, the object being to find first. Smith knew that in order for his American hounds to be classified as New World foxhounds, they had to compete against the long-established Old World packs. Smith was willing to conform as far as color and markings, but he was not willing to conform to the English hounds' hunting techniques, voice, size, and drive.

Alexander Henry Higginson and Harry Worcester Smith arrived at The Great Hound Match with hounds that could not have been more dissimilar. Higginson's English hounds were classically colored, classically carved, and classically trained. Smith's, while the "right" color, were scrawny and "snipey nosed" with overshot jaws. It remained to be seen which hound, American or English, could hunt longest, hardest, farthest, fastest—and which could kill a fox.

14

Day Six

Tuesday, November 7, 1905
Grafton Hunt's Third

"So swift was the pace cut out that not a single rider out of fifty-two, who had assembled at the meet, lived with the hounds at the end and few made even a pretense of doing so."
—ALLEN POTTS, *RICHMOND TIMES-DISPATCH*, WEDNESDAY, NOVEMBER 8, 1905

"BY GOD, THAT'S BEAUTIFUL MUSIC!" ALLEN POTTS SAID TO TERRY Dulany. They had parked their horses on top of a hill overlooking Cromwell's Run to watch Harry Worcester Smith's hounds chase a fox through the bottomland.

"That's got to be Sinner, Harry's leader," Terry Dulany said. She had taken a keen interest in Smith's hounds. American hounds ran in the Dulany family.

"That hound's voice is as rich as Caruso's," Potts said.

The morning had started once again at sunup at the Goose Creek Bridge. Slow at first, without a peep from the pack for over two hours, a hound named "Sue" and her cold-nosed friend "Sorry" finally caught a whiff, trailed for fifteen minutes and jumped a big red down below Chimney Hill at around 9:45. The girls called the rest of the pack in and from then on "Sinner," "Sin," "Spic," "Splash," "Simple," and "Sam" led the race. The fox had taken them all the way around the base of Chimney Hill where they checked for about fifteen minutes, then found his trail again and followed it for fifty fast minutes toward Atoka.

"Watch them fly," Potts said.

"That pace is too much for me," Terry Dulany admitted. "I don't want to kill my horse."

From their lookout, they could see the fox, his brush held high, about four hundred yards in front of Sinner and his gang. Behind the hounds, way behind them, were nine riders—the few remaining from the crowd that had gathered at the bridge hours ago.

It had been a hard-riding day from the very start. Right away a man named Bell, having come out from Baltimore on the weekend, tripped his horse up on a wall and down he went. Then Welby Carter, an Upperville native who should have known better, got hung up on a blind fence, and Tom Dougherty from Philly over-jumped a wall, coming off on the other side with a jolt.

The fact that the fox had taken the hounds on a goose chase around Chimney Hill and lost them for a few minutes when he'd rejoined his tracks had given the early field time to catch up. Grafton Abbot, Higginson's friend from Boston stationed on some high ground opposite the hill, viewed the fox and pointed him out to Master Smith who took his hounds in that direction; they soon found the trail and away they went again. In the next fifteen minutes, half of the field dropped out because of the pace, their horses used up. Seven people including Rozier Dulany tried, but it was a physical impossibility. "They ran as fast as greyhounds," Dr. McEachran said later in his judge's report. More riders dropped back at a treacherous in-and-out that turned across a lane with a wire-topped rail fence on the other side. After that, there were only about fifteen riders left. The hounds then flew through an open gate at the Fletcher farm on the other side of Ashby Gap Pike, but something sent the gate swinging and a man named Garrett from Massachusetts ran through it. His horse got hung up in the gate with his head on one side and his tail on the other. Luckily both were unscathed, but Garrett was forced to drop out too. Mal Richardson, who had had to pull up to avoid crashing into Garrett's horse, found himself in Mrs. Pierce's dangerous path. The gentle Amazon screamed "Out of the way!" rammed Richardson against the gate post, smashing his knee, squeezed past Garrett, and galloped on.

Plenty of people viewed the fox. Every hilltop in the neighborhood between Goose Creek and Cromwell's Run had a pod of riders perched there for the view. At one point, taking a shortcut across a hillside, several riders, including Master Smith and Charles McEachran, came to a precipice so steep it could safely be called a cliff. "I'll never do that again," McEachran said later of their descent. "Not in twenty more years of foxhunting."

They came to the Pierce farm near Atoka, which had been posted against trespassers, including foxhunters. The outlaw fox ignored the signs, probably hoping the hounds could read. They ignored it too. Mrs. Maddux, Mrs. Henderson, Harry Worcester Smith, Tom Pierce, Grafton Abbott, Dulany DeButts, Dr. McEachran, Dick Barrett, Allen Potts, and Mal Richardson were the only riders left to watch the hounds disappear into the distant hills.

The pack followed their fox back toward Middleburg, where they checked on the Fletcher farm. At this point, Jim Maddux, seeing that the pack had left their huntsman behind, took matters into his own hands and tried in vain for nearly an hour to put them on the fox's line. Hal Movius witnessed for the second time an outsider taking charge of Smith's pack and both times the outsider was serving as Smith's judge for The Match. Movius vowed silently to include the vagrant huntsmen-judges, which were clearly acting against the running rules, in his daily report.

Master Smith finally caught up and soon Mrs. Pierce, hill-topping nearby, saw the fox crossing a field of winter wheat. Smith blew his silver whistle and Sinner found the line once again.

"Hey, get out of that wheat," Smith called to a rider whom he did not know as they galloped after the pack. Smith had stuck to the outside of the wheat in deference to the farmer's tender winter crop and he instructed what remained of his field of riders to do the same. The man to whom Smith had called ignored him, running straight across, ahead of the Master. "You there!" Smith yelled again. Again the man ignored him. "You son-of-a-bitch, get off the goddam wheat!" Smith screamed.

"To hell with the wheat, keep up with your hounds," the man called back. "It's my wheat and I'll run across it if I want. Follow me!"

The field of riders, now numbering in the twenties again, went on the run of their lives—another twenty minutes of race riding. Soon neither stick nor spur could convince their horses to continue. One by one they dropped back again, "horses squeezed like lemons," Allen Potts wrote in his notebook for the next morning's *Times-Dispatch* report from the front. Smith, on The Cad, came to a boggy spot at Cromwell's Run and became mired in mud practically to his horse's hocks. By the time they were free, with the help of a handful of friends, the pack was again running without a Master or huntsman. Along with Smith, Marguerite and Morley Davis, Mrs. Pierce, judges Hal Movius and Jim Maddux, Leonard Ahl, Willy Fletcher, and Claude Hatcher were at last forced to give it up, their horses done in. A farmer told Smith that his little pack of thirteen American hounds had run their fox into its den under a rock ledge on Goose Creek and that's where they found them, one and all, gathered round baying at the creek bank.

The Grafton and the Middlesex Hunts had each had three days of hunting in The Match. Each had had a blank first day, each had had two good days with good scent; each had had spectacular runs, and each had put more than one fox to ground. But neither had had a kill. The foxes of both Loudoun and Fauquier Counties were showing their own stuff. It was proving easier said than done—to kill a wild Virginia fox.

15

The Amazons

"Well-behaved women rarely make history."
—Laurel Thatcher Ulrich

From Day One the women in The Match were phenomenal. Allen Potts, whose wife, the former Gertrude Rives, was Master *and* huntsman—the only woman huntsman in the United States at the time—of The Castle Hill Hounds outside Richmond, Virginia, included in his daily wires to the *Times-Dispatch* the progress of the eight or ten women who rode in The Match every day. Beginning with Terry Dulany's sensational jump the first day of The Match on her horse Welbourne Bachelor, Potts was clearly in awe of the Amazons riding to hounds that November.

Sidesaddle was still the only acceptable, presentable way for a woman to ride in company in 1905. Though Emily Ladenburg, a resident of Long Island and member of the Meadow Brook Hunt who also rode in The Match, tried to introduce culottes into polite society at Palm Beach in 1902, it was not until the 1930s that women were seen with any regularity having a leg on either side of her mount. Notwithstanding Annie Oakley, on the East Coast trousers were forbidden. Women still dressed in the Victorian high collars, poufy-bosomed dresses, flowing skirts with trains, and slippered feet. Remember, the modern bra was not yet patented. Women were allowed to dance and maybe ride a horse if both were well under control. A well-trained lady's hunter under sidesaddle was expected to canter at the speed of a fast walk.

Catherine De Medici takes credit in the sixteenth century for shifting her weight from perpendicular to her horse's spine to practically parallel, throwing her leg over the pommel, exposing her ankle and calf, and taking charge of her own charger. She is also credited with inventing and equipping her saddles with an additional lower pommel, the "second crutch." Prior to Catherine's daring accomplishment, a woman was seated either behind a man on a horse or alone on a donkey or pony on a padded saddle, a "sambue," with a platform for her feet. It took around a hundred years for the "modern" sidesaddle to take shape beginning in the first third of the nineteenth century with Jules Charles Pellier's third pommel—the "leaping horn"—which allowed women to dispense with the man. Now she could ride out alone or in a group, trot, canter, and even leap. Should she find herself in a tight spot out on the hunt field she could simultaneously squeeze her right leg against the upper crutch, and her left against the liberating leaping head in a sort of vice grip to stay in her tack. Elisabeth, Empress of Austria, was one of the first women to do so and she became famous when she visited England in 1876 to hunt with John, 5th Earl Spencer, and the Pytchley hounds.

The empress was a sensation. She had long, extraordinarily long, reddish-brown curly hair. She was five feet eight inches tall, towering for her time. Her complexion was impeccable, alabaster, flawless. She obsessed about her figure, maintaining an eighteen-inch waist all her life. She scandalized the hunting set by spurning petticoats; instead she had a chamois "second skin" made, into which she was sewn, beneath her gold-buttoned blue riding habit. She wore a high black hat with her hair carefully pinned beneath. It took an hour or two to prepare, but one can imagine that she finished the day's hunting without a hair out of place. To protect her complexion, she used a mixture of cold cream, camphor, and borax for her facial, as well as a strawberry ointment made from the juice of wild berries and Vaseline preserved with salicylic acid.[1]

And she could ride. The fourth of ten children, her daddy Duke Max, Maximilian Joseph of the Bavarian Hapsburgs, nicknamed her "Sisi" and taught her to ride. Sisi inherited her father's feel for a horse and his love for the circus, particularly the daring acrobatic riders. To teach Sisi a balanced seat, Max had sidesaddles made with reversible pommels so that she could practice riding on both the near and far sides, and for an added challenge, without a stirrup. "She had a knack," Franz Jebhart, her instructor at the Vienna Haute École, said of her.[2] She learned to hunt in Bavaria but decided to travel to England when she heard how hard and fast the

English hunters rode and jumped. She stayed near Earl Spencer's home in Northamptonshire and took the Pytchley Hunt by storm.

It was customary to appoint a "pilot" to hunt alongside a lady, particularly a lady of royalty, and Spencer appointed his groom, the hard-riding, philandering, fearless Bay Middleton, who acquiesced "just this once."[3] When he found that the empress could not only keep up but could ride and jump abreast of him and even better him over the Pytchley single and double "oxers"—those stout timber rails erected a few feet out from the cut-and-laid timber fences designed especially to contain the enormous oxen raised in Northamptonshire at the time—he became her permanent escort and her lover. Besides the oxers there were also "bullfinches" to clear, brush-covered fences erected across ten-foot-wide gullies at the bottom of the Pytchley watersheds through which a horse had to be brave enough to plow since most were too high to jump. The oxers and bullfinches were enough to stall or at least give pause to even the best riders. These were "the greatest days of English foxhunting," . . . no wire, to tarmac, no cars, no plow . . . "Every inch of land was pasture, good galloping English grass which stock had grazed for centuries."[4] To ride with the Pytchley, a girl had to be not only brave but good. Spencer paid her the highest of compliments: "She was as good as she looked."[5]

The French called them "*Amazones*," these daring women who rode to hounds with sporting sagacity. Those who rode in the haute école, the art of manège, were "equestriennes," but those who rode out across the countryside were Amazons. They belonged to the aristocracy, the bourgeoisie, whereas the equestriennes belonged to the "demi-monde" of actresses, dancers, and circus performers. Today women who prefer riding sidesaddle are still called Amazons.

There were plenty of men who didn't approve of women on the hunt field. Belle Beach couched a fair warning in a statement of pride when in 1900 she wrote, "When a woman hunts, she enters a masculine field of sport and in the hunting-field she is meeting men on their own grounds and on even terms."[6] George Underhill, also writing in 1900, didn't entirely trust the Amazons or their mounts. "The habit of mounting ladies on thoroughbreds, which have been out of racing stables, is dangerous to a degree bordering on crime." But, he concedes, "To tell a lady that she should not hunt until she can ride is like forbidding a little boy to go into the water until he can swim." He recommends early training of mind and body, preferably by a man: "The nervous system should be educated during girlhood . . . a strong nerve, fine hands, and a firm seat are important . . . the best are taught by their fathers when they were little girls, though I know women who were taught by their husbands."[7] Others were just resigned to women on the hunt field, "When women ride they generally ride like the very devil!"[8]

A good many hunting men turned to their hounds to understand the presence of women in their hunt field. Peter Beckford, author of the early and revered *Thoughts on Hunting: In a Series of Letters to a Friend* (1781) advises against naming a puppy "Madam" in case one must berate her in the field, "Madam, you d——d bitch."

Alice Hayes, writing in 1903, believed that the distinction between mounted men and women is not the horse, nor nerve, but their tack—what she calls "the tyranny of the side-saddle"—when she writes, "the great difference between men and women is that the former ride the horse; the latter, the saddle."[9] The rider's balance has to be perfect; her spine should be aligned with the horse's. Sidesaddles must be properly fitted for the woman as well as the horse. Each must be essentially custom made. A sidesaddle is heavy, thirty pounds or more, often counterweighted on the far side for balance. It is bigger, requiring a bigger, better behaved, more expensive horse. Think of it as the Ginger Rogers school of equitation: dance like Fred Astaire, only backward and in high heels. Esther Stace set the world's record jumping sidesaddle, clearing 6'6" in 1918 at the Sydney Easter Games.[10]

Mrs. Amy Charlotte Bewickle Menzies, writing in 1913, has much to say about everything from etiquette to attire for the Amazon. She has some pet peeves to predicate and, in the manner of a good country Englishwoman, takes no prisoners:

"Not long ago I saw quite a well-known follower of a South Country pack get off her horse to lead it over an awkward place, and behold! An expanse of large black-and-white check breeches, not in their first youth, and when I explain the individual was not of slender proportions I feel the picture is complete."[11]

For one's hair, Mrs. Menzies advises pins, pins, pins: "It is difficult to prevent it sticking out like the handle of a jug, but it can be done with a little management." As for boots, "if there still exists such a thing as elastic-sided boots, burn them." One will need a good strong crop, "a flimsy thing will double up or do something foolish." And to guard against a wind-blown complexion she recommends "a dessert spoonful of raw mustard or ammonia applied." She advises against corsets on the hunt field: "no woman looks well on horseback in tight corsets . . . the stoutness is there be it shoved up or shoved down." If she finds herself growing fat she advises a diet not unlike the South Beach: "avoid sugar, milk, bread, rice, potatoes, all roots and starchy food; eat instead lean meat, vegetables grown in the air and light, cauliflower, French beans, asparagus, spinach and so on."

While admitting that "the unwritten laws and etiquette of the hunting field are rigid," Mrs. Menzies ascribed to and evidently practiced the favorite steeplechaser's mantra, "throw your heart over and your horse will follow." Nor is she averse to falling off every now and then. "Nothing gives you confidence like a good-natured fall—one when neither you nor your mount are much the worse; you have not broken your horse's back, and he has not trodden on your face, or any little pleasantry of that kind." If you should perhaps knock your teeth out she advises a quick replacement, "I have always maintained it is part of our duty towards our neighbor to make ourselves as little repulsive as possible . . . it is your duty to your neighbor to buy some new teeth."

The Match was an incomparable opportunity for foxhunting women to show their stuff. Allen Potts reported that they were all "crack" riders on "crack" hunters. Mrs. Westmoreland Davis, future first lady of Virginia, brought a string of six hunters including "O.K." and "P.D.Q"; Mrs. Thomas L. Pierce brought "Nassaquag," "Bruce," and "John Peel"; Mrs. Laden-burg came from Long Island and rode one of Mr. Ahl's hunters, "Tapps"; Miss Dulany from Upperville, Virginia was on "Welbourne Bachelor"; Mrs. Henderson rode "The Wizard"; and Mrs. Grafton Abbott was on her clever bay hunter, "Crugor." Alexander Henry Higginson, in his 1931 autobiography *Try Back*, writes about the Amazons in The Match, "I like to remember the way those gallant ladies rode in the field—stopping for nothing, turning aside for nothing . . . riding 'straight for the sea.'"

16

On the Nature of Scent

"Nought so queer, 'cept a woman."

—Mr. Jorrocks

SCENT IS A REPELLENT, AN ATTRACTANT, A STENCH, A PERFUME, A PINE cone, a skunk, lavender or feces. To catch one is to sniff, to sneeze, to inhale and taste, exhale, concentrate, test the wind, follow your nose. If you stick your nose where it doesn't belong you may smell a rat. But stop, smell the roses, or a wedge of Stilton or Courvoisier from a *snif*ter. A human's sense of smell is a complex system analogous to that of language. Can't we assume that a dog's is too?[1] A dog, sniffing five times a second, sifts odors through a "labyrinth of paper-thin bones—the olfactory recess— lined with millions of scent receptors" making his sense of smell "up to 100,000 times more acute than a human's."[2] And consider the horse's long Roman nose filled also with scent receptors ready to detect friends and foe far more frequently than we. Many foxhunters acknowledge that their horse sees—smells—the fox long before he or she does. Hunting takes a fair imagination, some trust, and a little blind faith. Between a man and his horse, the hound and the fox, some will excel where others will fail. Venery is a game, a war game, a puzzle and a gas. It's "something of the whimsical combined with an eeriness boarding on the supernatural."[3] It's a science. But mostly it's an art.

When Tolstoy's hero, Nikolai Rostov, decided to go hunting one September morning, while home on leave from the Russian War of 1812, he called his favorite Bolshoi hound, Milka, summoned his huntsman Danilo, and invited his father. Nor could he refuse his sister and brother. A party of fifty-four hounds, six hunt attendants and whippers-in, plus forty Borzois and their kennelmen—all together a hundred and thirty dogs and twenty horsemen—set off and traveled two *versts* (a little over a half-mile) to a copse where a she-wolf had recently moved her cubs. "It was an unsurpassable morning for hunting: it was as if the sky were melting and sinking to the earth without any wind . . . the air in the kitchen garden looked wet and black and glistened like poppy-seed . . . there was a smell of decaying leaves and of dog." Recent nights had been cold. "The wooded ravines and the copses, which at the end of August had still been green islands amid black fields and stubble, had become golden and bright-red islands amid the green of winter rye." The hunting party spread out. The huntsman cried, "*Ulyulyulyu! Ulyulyulyu!*" Tolstoy knew well of what he wrote. There was *War*, but this is *Peace*—a kind of war within peace.[4]

Why was it an unsurpassable morning for hunting? Why wait until fall? True, the fox and wolf cubs in Tolstoy's countryside had begun to disperse by September, and the same is true in Virginia and in England, but it was and still is for the elusive scent that the hunters wait—for the air to cool and "melt into the earth." For the earth to exhale. Fixture cards mirror scent.

Foxhunters in moist grassy Great Britain brag about their good scenting conditions—the earth seems always to be exhaling moisture. Therein was exactly the reason for Higginson's challenge, which resulted in The Match. Higginson held that the same hound that hunted so well in England could hunt in America. Smith reasoned that a different land, a different climate, a different topography and soil type called for an altogether different hound. Smith and his followers felt that America and England were not, nor would they ever be, equal, an oft-uttered statement that held a different meaning for every person who spoke it at the turn of the twentieth century.

The challenge accepted, it was no accident that Smith and Higginson chose Virginia to hold their Match. The mid-Atlantic coast is the best foxhunting country in the United States precisely because of its rolling topography, its karst geology, dirt, types of trees, and vast native grasslands in the Piedmont and across the Blue Ridge into the Shenandoah Valley, where springs feed ever-branching rivers like the Potomac, the James, the Rappahannock, and the Shenandoah. Rolling and open, yes, but England it is not. The Appalachians, the oldest mountains on the continent, are never far from the east coast and their dry, scrubby, scrappy foothills are a challenge for any hunter or hound. East of the foothills lies the Atlantic seaboard's gently sloping Piedmont, a geological feature untethered by state lines anticipating the fall line along coastal plains stretching from New Jersey to the Carolinas and Georgia. The Piedmont's tempting temperate climate, particularly the mid-Atlantic region in Virginia and Maryland, home of the first foxhunting clubs in America, makes a huntsman and his hounds salivate.

Though the red fox is native to Canada and New England, he was imported to the Southern colonies late in the eighteenth century and his comings and goings along the Eastern Seaboard have been well documented. Larry Birdsong writes of the red fox's advance from Maryland through Pennsylvania, Virginia, and on to East Georgia "slowly but steadily pursuing a Southwesterly direction, parallel with the mountain chain running through the Middle States . . . keeping pace with the depleting, waste-land process of cotton culture," in 1830.[5] Joel Chandler Harris, author of the famous and infamous Uncle Remus stories, wrote "The First Red Fox in Georgia" for *The American Field* in 1892, describing the advance of the red fox, his displacement of the native gray in the process, and the different means by which a huntsman and his hounds had to pursue the crafty interloper. "The gentlemanly and ladylike gray" that were native to his home in Putnam County "always had the politeness to double on their trail, going at a comfortable pace, and keeping well within hearing of an enthusiastic sportsman." But the newcomers ran straight, strong, and far. It was soon after this that Georgia hunters began breeding a different hound, one that could "cope" with the reds, "dogs with speed, grit, bottom and noses more keenly alive to the situation." These newer breeds were the Birdsong and Henry hounds from Virginia, stock from which Harry Worcester Smith chose his foundation sires and bitches.

To exactly what situation need these noses be keenly alive? Is there a scientific formula for scent? In the fall, on those crisp mornings when the air is cooler than the earth, when the blue hazes of summer dissipate and there is a contrast to the light that turns the fence lines sharp and black, scent is practically palpable. Even a human can smell it. At other times on bright sunny mornings with high clouds, there is no scent to speak of. Why? When and where should a huntsman cast his hounds? What *exactly* is scent? Surely science can answer these questions. It's something hunters and huntsmen, amateur and professional, have been trying to pin down since, well, probably since man stood on two legs to draw his bow.

Vulpes vulpes, the American red fox, has a caudal scent gland at the top of his tail, four on each foot pad, and another in his anal gland. Part of why he is thought to be so clever is how, when, and why he sprays or hides his scent. His adroitness at covering his tracks is the one trait that has lifted his reputation from that of a simple varmint to a trick-ster of mythological proportion. Some writers like P. C. Spink believe that a fox "knows whether scent is good or bad and runs through soiled ground, flocks of sheep, rolls in muck in order to counter his own scent."[6] Whether Mr. Spink asked the fox if he knew if the scent was good that day may be beside the point, since many have seen a fox do exactly those things while being chased by a pack of hounds. Foxhunting literature is full of accounts of foxes "creeping" along "on tiptoe" as slowly as pos-sible with hounds on their tails just to keep from stirring up their own scent. "On such occasions, the cry of hounds will be queer, as if they were uncertain as to whether they are right."[7] It is not only how a fox runs, but through what they run that makes a scent. Bruised grass and weeds over which a fox will run are both blamed and valued for bad and good scent. "Scent is blamed for virtually every bad day of hunting, not to mention losses, checks, huntsmen's and field masters' mistakes, heel lines, overruns, and changes to fresh game."[8]

On the nature of scent, Beckford quotes Somervile (everybody quotes Somervile),[9] Birdsong quotes Beckford, Harris quotes Birdsong, and on and on. Many a great hound-man has taken a stab at it. Somervile thinks that scent lies in the air; Beckford disagrees—it's in the soil. Birdsong says that the peculiar odor that a fox "has the power of ejecting at plea-sure," resembles the crown imperial, a lily native to Turkey and Afghani-stan.[10] Redmond Stewart, founder and huntsman for Green Spring Valley Hounds in Maryland early in the twentieth century, learned from experi-ence that hounds running upwind find good scent; that dry leaves turned over on a fox's line spoil scent; that a south wind on the mid-Atlantic coast is bad; that a sudden and great cold front is bad; and that a fox could (and would) obliterate his scent by crossing a soft slimy plowed field. He also learned that it is useless to hunt on a nice frosty morning and that a warm wind thawing a hard-frozen ground does nothing whatsoever for scent.[11] Joseph Thomas admits that "the oddities of scent are apparently inexplicable."[12] It comes down to this: "melting conditions are usually good; freezing the reverse." Thomas gives a good quasi-scientific definition of scent: "a mixture of volatile oils together with aqueous skin secretions which in their gaseous state enable hounds to detect and hunt their quarry." Now we're getting somewhere.

In 1933 H. M. Budgett decided to capture the nature of scent once and for all in his "Apparatus for the Determination of Scent Conditions."[13] First he dug a hole a foot deep and connected it via a pipe laid in a trench to a drain tester "some distance away" into which he dropped a smoke bomb and presumably stood back. "Smoke came oozing out of the hole in a dense cloud which obscured the view of what was happening at the bottom of the hole." Rats. However, he did notice "spirals of smoke actually being sucked into the earth round the edges of the hole." He notes that air temperature at the time of the experiment was seven degrees above that of the ground. What now? Budgett "at once commandeered the services of a man with a spade," and went around the neighborhood digging holes. Alas, "always the ground sucked the smoke down." When he tried on days when the ground temperature was higher than that of the air, there was always a breeze. (Could it be that the reverse in temperature *caused* the breeze?) Poor Budgett "reluctantly decided that this was not a reliable method of testing scenting conditions." Not to worry, he modified his contraption by connecting a cone with a tube to a box over the hole in an attempt to catch a breeze coming up or down the cone. No luck. Then he cut a rectangle in a cardboard circle, captured a spider's web with some sticky stuff on a glass cylinder, put it in the tube, and found that "when currents of air were rising from the earth, the spider's web bulged outward, when they were sinking into the ground, it was sucked inward." Cool. But the spider-web-diaphragm lay "bulging out when the scent was bad." This begs the question, if he knew that the scent was bad, why did he need the Apparatus? All was not lost;

he convinced himself that "IN FACT THE EARTH BREATHES." Eureka! Well done, Budgett.

But wait, Budgett didn't rest on those laurels. He built "The Electric Scent Indicator" consisting of two thermometers at each end of a wooden rod, which could be jabbed into the ground at will. Press a button and an electric current detects the difference between the air and ground temperature and a battery-operated needle points left or right, indicating good or bad scent. He even made a portable one on a walking stick. Alas, the wooden stick acted as an insulator and hounds could be long gone by the time it registered. When next he built one into a bronze walking stick he burned his hand. Lesson: "If the instruments show that the earth is warmer than the air and the needle of the indicator moves across to the left, there is quite certain to be good scent, providing the quarry has not gained too long a start." Gentlemen, hold onto your hounds until the needle moves!

Henry Tegner might have the last word in hunting literature on the nature of scent: "Scent appears to be one of those intriguing phenomena of nature which has so far successfully defied this maniac-technological age of micro-analysis and computers."[14] Tegner had his own scentimeter, "a little Australian Terrier named Waltzing Mathilda.... How quickly she runs the line," when he lets her out the back door tells him "whether scent will make hounds scream that day or cause them to remain comparatively silent." Go Matti!

So the nature of scent has something to do with relative humidity, wind speed and direction, barometric pressure, soil content and contour, vegetation and crops, and a great deal to do with the ratio of ground temperature to air. Fine, but what about the personalities involved? There's the man, his horse—a bitchy mare, an uppity gelding, or an overpowering stallion—a pack of hounds—say fifty bitches and dogs each with his or her own personality—and the fox in any order or combination. Now it gets complicated. As Spink puts it, "the number of permutations possible resulting from the interaction of twenty or more factors is potentially very large."[15] It's like trying to write a formula for love, or maybe breast milk.

We've come to the place where art and science part company. Here in the gorse or the copse, the thicket or the covert—where the huntsman and his hounds may or may not be in the right place at the right time—this is where tradition, knowledge, intuition, gumption, faith, and common sense meet. This is also where differing hunting techniques championed by differing traditions compounded by everything from patriotism to patrimony can fester into a full-fledged battle. The Great Hound Match was, if anything, a fight between two men who came down on opposite sides of a formula each had written in his own mind for the most successful method of hunting a fox. Should the huntsman guide his hounds, as was the English method and for which Alexander Henry Higginson's English foxhound was bred, or should the huntsman let his hounds guide him, the American method for which English hounds were crossed with Welsh, Irish, blood, coon, and you-name-its to produce Harry Worcester Smith's American foxhound? It almost matters not. Regardless of the players, without scent there is no hunt.

Isaac Bell, the famous American-born huntsman for the Irish Galway Blazers, Kilkenny and South and West Wilts early in the twentieth century, wrote the fictional hunting manual *Foxiana*, in which he explains the importance of introducing the hound, any hound, to a pure and carefully guarded scent. Told from the perspective of each hunting participant—huntsman, hound, follower, master—Bell's first chapter, "A Hunting Day," is from the huntsman's point of view, illustrating his shrewd understanding of every nuance of the meet and their scenting chances for the day:

"Looks a rare sort of day. Bet there's a scent. Coming along hounds were raking on, determined looking, and their mouths shut tight. Never saw the thorn look blacker. Everything smelling so strong. See how the smoke hangs. I can smell the colonel's cigar from across the road.

"Let's move hounds away from the exhausts of these motor cars. It makes them sneeze—gets into their coats and all helps to foil scent. I can smell that iodoform. That's where I dressed Caroline's cut foot. Forgot to wash it off this morning. We want no other scent with us than 'Fox.' I do hate the smell of bath salts and hair wash. Delicate organ a hound's nose, can't be too careful.

"Blackthorn Gorse the first draw. What a good day to 'hear.' Listen to the clatter of the horses on the stony lane! The slamming of the gate. The barking of that collie. *And* that man driving cattle. Pity our first covert's down-wind of it all!"

Bell's fictional huntsman watches every move each hound makes while hacking to the meet, their mouths shut tight to inhale each passing molecule across their "scentimeters." They are determined-looking. All business. He notices the peculiar contrast to the light that turns the thorn hedges black, which speaks to the old saying among foxhunters, "Good scent when fences and hedges look sharp and black, poor scent when there is a blue haze." He notices chimney smoke hanging about. Back when locomotives belched steam and every household had a fire in the morning, hunters often watched the smoke for telltale signs of scent. And Bell is worried about his hounds' sensitive noses being contaminated with "the colonel's" cigar smoke, noxious automobile fumes (this was written in 1929 when people were beginning to show up for meets in vans), various bath salts and perfumes, and the iodine he had neglected to wash from an injured hound's foot.[16] Can you hear the horses clattering on the cobblestones, the slamming of the gate? Sound carries so well on such a still, dense morning as this, one may as well be underwater. Bell has captured all of a huntsman's senses and shown us how he uses them to guide and follow his hounds. He was famous for his intuition and foresight. He believed in a hound's intelligence. He knew his hounds and he knew their prey. As the Old Blue Pye says, "The huntsman knows my name and he knows that I know that he knows it, too."[17]

The red fox is muse for the best tellers of tall tales told. Stories of famous chases have filled the pages of hunting journals since, well, since man stood on two legs to paint his cave. Joel Chandler Harris tells the story of a chase, "perhaps the most famous in the hunting annals of middle Georgia," after "Old Napper," a red fox known not because he liked to sleep, but for the estate where he made his home in 1848. On a fine morning after a warm rain "twenty or thirty hunters assembled having with them fifty hounds" to catch the Old Napper, who had foiled their dogs long enough. Some eight hours and around sixty miles later they finally captured and killed the fox, having also killed three horses and "winded" four in the process. Then there's the story of "Old Whitey," a fox with a solid white tail who ran a hundred hounds and some two hundred and fifty riders for eight hours from one end of northwestern Virginia to the other and back again before he was caught and killed. "Carpenters left their unfinished houses, colored hands quit shucking corn, wagoners unhitched their horses and left their teams standing in the road to join in this wonderful foxhunt." Old Whitey took them on a wild chase to the Rappahannock River and back again: "From the Piney [Mountains] he swam Carter's Run, passed through the Free State and made straight for the Little Cobler, then he struck for Big Cobler and thence to Henson's Ford on the Rappahannock River . . . running for eight hours . . . in full cry from start to finish."[18]

Those were real foxes; then there are the fictional foxes. Remember Joel Chandler Harris's Br'er Rabbit hollering, "Please, Br'er fox, don't fling me in dat brier-patch!" Harris's retelling of an oral tradition among Native Americans and African slaves may be one of the few times in the history of storytelling when the fox was outsmarted. Reynard is one of the oldest antiheros in the history of western storytelling.[19] In literature, along with the good company of King Arthur, Charlemagne, the Trojans, and the Norsemen, Reynard's adventures have reached the stratospheric literary designation of "cycle." In France he is Renard, the Flemish knew him as Reinaert or Reinaerde, in Germany Reinhart or Reineke, in Italy Rainardo, and in the earliest Latin Reinardus, written sometime in the middle of the twelfth century. Chaucer included him in his "Nun's Priest's Tale." Renard, the little French fox, is believed to have been created by Pierre de St. Cloud, taken from medieval fantastic tales and written down in 1175 as moral and political allegories. "Renard became the personification of hypocrisy, deceit and evil—a symbol of sin, the Devil in disguise."[20] Renard's quarrel with the wolf Isengrim in a kingdom ruled by the lion Noble is unresolved until 1270 when the allegory evolves and Renard takes over Noble's throne. Accused by Isengrim of raping his wife, Renard escapes. Vice conquers Virtue.

In foxhunting literature he is variously known as Dan Russel (from Chaucer), Charles James or Charlie (after a non-hunting Whig caricatured by the Tories), Sir Russet, Red Jacket, Tod Fox, Sir or Master Dan, and Wiley. Hitler was known as the "Black Fox." D. H. Lawrence's novella *The Fox* is a good example of characterizing as vulpine those least admirable of human traits. When a young Cornish soldier named Henry, on leave from his unit during the Great War, visits his family's abandoned farmstead where he finds two young women trying to make a go of it, he is curiously attracted to one of the girls, March, over whom he seems to hold some sort of psychological control. While trying hard to raise poultry for market, the girls have been dogged by a local fox who keeps raiding the coop and stealing chickens right from under their noses. They take turns guarding the coop with a shotgun to little avail. March comes face to face with the thief one evening, looks him straight in the eye, but can't seem to shoot him. When Henry arrives, the girls have two foxes on their hands. He decides to marry March and take over the farm himself. He hunts her as though she is prey. He looks at her and she feels "the same sly, taunting, knowing spark leap out of his eyes, as he turned his head aside, and fall into her soul, as it had fallen from the dark eyes of the fox." Henry walks "with his head thrust forward," his eyes are "wise and childish . . . strangely clear," he "saw everything and examined everything," an "invisible smile . . . like a cunning little flame gleamed on his face." He is, like a fox, at once comical and cunning, whimsical and wicked, eerily evil. As Lawrence foreshadows in the novella's first paragraph, "Unfortunately, things did not turn out well," for the girls.

Thomas Wolfe, that master of autobiographical fiction, used fox mythology to describe his fictional editor, Foxhall Morton Edwards, in *Look Homeward Angel*: "O, guileful Fox, how innocent in guilefulness and in innocence how full of guile, in all directions how strange-devious, in all strange-deviousness how direct! Too straight for crookedness, and for envy too serene, too fair for blind intolerance, too just and seeing and too strong for hate, too honest for base dealing, too high for low suspiciousness, too innocent for all the scheming tricks of swarming villainy."[21]

Perhaps the best example of a fox's cleverness and craftiness is a true story, one for the annals of natural history, an eye-witness account of a fox ridding himself of fleas. Jan Blan Van Urk quotes Reginald Innes Pocock (F.L.S., F.Z.S., F.R.A.I., F.R.S., Natural History Editor of *The Field* and assistant of the Zoological Department at the British Museum), who watched a fox do an extraordinary thing: "Taking a small tuft of wool or piece of wood a fox will slowly sink himself, tail first, into a pond and thus gradually drive the fleas forward until the last refuge is the wool or wood on the surface of the water. The fox then sets this adrift, teaming with parasites and keeping clear of it (as it floats away) lands on the bank and makes off."[22]

It's hard to remember, with the many human traits to which he is assigned in the hype and glory of mythology, that the fox in biological terms is simply a very successful predator, an adaptable competitive omnivore who only lives as long as his teeth hold out. His range can be a small suburban neighborhood or five square miles of farmland. He is the consummate locavore, surviving on everything from worms to apples to rabbits or persimmons. Mice are a favorite. He has the reputation of being a "loner" because he only eats prey smaller than himself and doesn't need to hunt in a pack. His tail is about a third of his nearly fifty-inch body length and because he can spring and fly with the best of the world's mousers he often looks much larger and longer than reality. He will stop and stand and look you in the eye then lope off unfazed. He can make himself visible or invisible in a blink; he is a magician. The fox has been personified, humanized, and anthropomorphized with abandon until the poor guy, though maintaining his dignity, has very little privacy. An adult vixen may mark her territory with urine over a hundred and fifty times in a twenty-four-hour period. But that's not the extent of her scent. Consider where she runs, how quickly she runs, when she decides to run and when to walk on tiptoe. In fact, a vixen with young is said not to have any scent at all and neither do her cubs. For her mate's scent look to the sky for stacked clouds with black bottoms on a day in late fall when a new snow is melting. Find a wet spot with plenty of fragrant grasses or a copse with a moist floor of rotting leaves. Stay away from plowed earth and dry leaves. Hunt in the morning before the sun is high or in the evening when the "race between darkness and good scent begins."[23] Follow a good huntsman. Stay out of the way and keep your mouth shut.

Good luck.

17

Week Two

November 8–14, 1905

HAVING BEEN ON THE FRONT PAGE OF THE *RICHMOND TIMES-DISPATCH* for the first seven days of November, The Match took a backseat to more pressing matters, namely politics; Tuesday, November 7, was election day for Virginia and, amid "almost paralyzing apathy," the Democrats swept the state, placing Claude Swanson into the governor's office. The front pages were also headlined with the ongoing riots and revolution in Russia and scandals at Tammany Hall in New York City's election. Nevertheless, the visitors to Upperville and Middleburg were still going strong, completely absorbed in their own tests of strength, endurance, guts, and nerve.

As usual in November, Virginia's weather turned in the second week. The first few days of The Match had been almost balmy with highs in the sixties (°F) and lows in the upper forties. On Wednesday, November 8, the temperature did not reach fifty and the night had been below freezing, making conditions for foxhunting just about perfect. Thursday the 9th was cold and windy but there was a frost that night leaving ice on the creeks on Friday the 10th. There was a full "frosty" moon on Sunday the 12th.

These are the exact conditions to which the northern foxhunters had been looking forward. The earth had been heated from October's and early November's warm days and now that there was a frost almost every night, when the sun climbed the next morning and hit cold air on top of warm earth, scent rose like the aroma from a pot of simmering stew. And also like a pot of simmering stew, as the second week progressed tensions in the rival hunt clubs rose, accompanied by a bitterness destined to stick in the contestants' craws for the near and distant future.

The running rules for the match stated (in italics) that *"The killing of the fox [was] to be the test,"* and went on to clarify: "If this cannot be accomplished in two weeks, the judges may continue the trials until same has been accomplished, or award the trials to the pack which, in their opinion, has done the best work with that object in view." In other words, unless a fox was killed, the contest would become as subjective as an Olympic ice skating or gymnastic competition, a dance-off, a beauty contest.

Two complaints had been lodged with the judges by the beginning of the second week. Harry Worcester Smith had not yet been given credit for his claim that his hounds had run a fox to ground on November 2. That was the day the hounds ran away from the Master, huntsmen, field, and staff with the exception of Claude Hatcher, who found them at an abandoned house near the quarry. The second complaint was from Higginson, claiming that the Grafton pack had been hunted by "outsiders," other than Smith, which the running rules prohibit stating, "The packs are to be hunted by their Masters or huntsmen," but the rules go on to say, "or in case of accident by someone duly appointed by them." The claims were to be settled at a meeting on Sunday, November 12. Just how long The Match was to continue was also at issue. Smith claimed that two weeks hunting meant seven days each; Higginson felt that six days of hunting for each pack were plenty.

On the first day of the second week twenty-six hunts were represented from the United States, Canada, and the British Isles: Middlesex, Grafton, Myopia, Brunswick, and Norfolk of Massachusetts; Piedmont, Keswick, Deep Run, Cameron Run, Blue Ridge, Warrenton, Orange County, Loudoun, and Mr. Miller's Hounds of Virginia; Meadow Brooke, Virginia-Carolina Westchester, and Essex of New York; Radnor, Allendale, and Brandywine of Pennsylvania; the Montreal Hunt of Canada, the Meath of Ireland and Mr. Fernie's Hounds of England.

The Middlesex Hunt was winning the popularity contest in Middleburg, most likely due to Alexander Henry Higginson's gentlemanly appearance and manners. "Master Higginson has made himself very popular throughout the valley," Potts reported in the *Times-Dispatch*. There were plenty of dinners given almost every night and "a score of country houses" in both counties had "practically kept open house for the entertainment of the Northern visitors." On days the Middlesex was out, and not only when the weather was fine, upwards of fifty people showed, not only to ride but to follow in buggies as best they could. On days the Grafton hounds were out, crowds were in the twenties—the die-hards, the speed demons, the daredevils.

Herein lies one aspect of the debate that brought about The Match in the first place. One camp, the Middlesex, treated the sport as a fast-paced game of chance with a good amount of galloping, a chance to view a fox or two, possibly even a kill, and an opportunity to watch a professional huntsman at his work managing and hunting his hounds. The other camp, the Grafton followers, understood that foxhunting should be approached with utter abandon, that the hounds, not the huntsman, hunted the fox and that if you couldn't keep up you would, and should, be left behind. In essence, the Middlesex hunted to ride while Grafton rode to hunt.

On Wednesday the 8th, Middlesex's fourth day out, the meet was at the Fred Farm on the Pot House Road just north of Middleburg. Forty-two riders turned out for "almost perfect" hunting conditions. Hounds hunted down Waquepin Creek and over the Dillion, Nichols, and Duffey farms. They jumped a fox on the creek, which ran them through a flock of turkeys, checking them briefly, but they found the line again and ran him to ground under an abandoned stone house on the Dudley farm. Several followers saw the hounds flying with heads up not fifty yards behind their fox before he dove for cover under the house. At one point during the run, a farmer fixing his leaky roof abandoned his project, jumped down, threw a saddle on a cob and took off after the pack. "Well, my family may die of pneumonia," the man later told Potts, "but a man can't sit on top of a house and nail shingles while fox hounds are giving tongue around the neighborhood." Mrs. Pierce rode astride that day (a scandalous position for a lady anywhere but Middleburg) on her new horse Champion, which she had purchased from Courtland Smith, Harry Worcester Smith's brother who was stationed at Oakley and hadn't been riding because he had broken his collarbone the day before the match started. Tragically, Champion, an ex-steeplechase horse, overreached at a rail fence that day and tore a tendon, throwing Mrs. Pierce onto a pile of rocks and chipping her front tooth. The intrepid (or crazy) Amazon sent for another horse, mounted with a bleeding mouth and rode off to find the hounds. Will Edwards, a Middlesex whip on his appropriately named horse, "Trouble," crash-landed on the other side of a wall and Hal Movius, following too closely, landed square on top of Will and Trouble. "It looked like the boy [Edwards] would surely be killed," Potts later reported, adding, "these two falls completed the casualties for the day." He also reported that Jim Maddux's horse, "Wade," was rendered lame.

Thursday, November 9 was Grafton's fourth day out and equally eventful. They met at 6:30 a.m. at Zulla, an estate ten miles south of Upperville to hunt a new territory on the road to The Plains. It was cold, dry, and windy. Only fourteen people turned out, all of the Grafton persuasion except of course for Mrs. Pierce, this time on her very reliable hunter "Searchlight." Everyone predicted that the scent would be lousy. Master Higginson showed up in a buggy, unable to ride because he had sent his horses by an alternate route and they had apparently gotten lost. But the scent wasn't so bad. Hounds began drawing at 7:15 and jumped a fox at 8:30, ran it nine miles only to run square into John Townsend's Orange County Hunt out of The Plains running the same fox. For a while they joined forces and ran together, but Smith soon gathered up his hounds and returned to Oakley, vowing to hunt till sundown. At 3:30 that afternoon they did indeed jump another fox on Cromwell's Run, probably the same one the Middlesex had jumped on Saturday, and ran it to ground at the ford on Goose Creek. The only riders up at the end were Smith, Rozier Dulany, Hal Movius, and Claude Hatcher. In the course of the day Paul Whitin had been trapped under his hunter, St. Michael, when it fell over a rail fence. At the end of the day, to Higginson's objections, Smith appointed Morley Davis as his new judge since Jim Maddux had been called away more or less permanently.

Twenty-six riders and a dozen buggies turned out in Middleburg on Friday, November 10 for Middlesex's fifth day hunting. After a long hack to a new territory several miles east of Middleburg near Aldie, Cotesworth cast the hounds at Dover. "Hounds ran so slowly all were able to keep up," Potts reported. They checked at Triplett's Hill, were cast again several times going toward Marble Quarry, found an old trail, and jumped a fox, which ran a short distance to its hole in the middle of Triplett's field. There was some doubt as to whether there indeed was a fox. A Mr. Rawlings and his friend Mr. Haxall who were out that day wrote a letter to the judges stating that they "saw one of the hunt servants at the den, hounds not tonguing at all, horns brought the hounds." Smith's new judge Davis "was absent from 10 a.m. to 2 p.m." according to the judges' report.

And then came Saturday.

It was Grafton's fifth day. Very cold. Scent reported as "fair." Claude Hatcher and Charles Eastman whipped in for Smith. The meet was at 7:30 at Mountsville. Higginson hadn't yet arrived, but that was nothing new so Smith set off promptly at half past the hour. Just before they left, word came that Higginson had been arrested for trespassing.

Allen Potts reported that "Mr. Higginson drove to the meet but was unable to follow Grafton hounds on account of having been arrested by Amos Payne over whose lands he inadvertently rode a few days ago," and Potts went on to explain Higginson's version of the story: that a man named Amos Payne was his accuser; that Higginson had been fined $100 and refused to pay; that Payne threatened to have the whole field arrested; that, in order to spare his friends' embarrassment, Higginson agreed to pay $50, saying to Mr. Payne, "I thank you for the splendid Virginia hospitality you have extended to me, a stranger, and I want to say to you that if you ever come to Massachusetts I will gladly have you ride over my lands and will promise not to have you arrested." According to Higginson, "Payne pocketed the money and rode off."

His opponent's arrest didn't stop Smith from hunting all day Saturday. Hounds were cast at Mount's farm and immediately found a fox. A farmer saw the fox; then he saw three. It must have been a fox conspiracy—they had discussed it over rabbit dinner the previous evening. They were sick to death of being chased every day for over a week, one day by big bruising hound dogs packed together like cigars in a box, the next by half-crazed wild animals resembling coyotes. They decided to get together and flummox those foxhounds.

It worked. The hounds were flustered, unable to decide which fox to chase. Smith used his whistle to put them on a single line, which they chased for an hour all the way to Oatlands, home of William Corcoran Eustis, near Leesburg. Halfway there, the hounds disappeared. The entire pack, without a trace. No one in the field heard them or saw them for an hour and a half. Smith later claimed that he had ridden around the countryside searching for his hounds, talking to "colored boys" on the roads, and deduced that they had run into a gulley heading south then turned around and ran north while the field, led by Smith, continued south, against the wind that carried the hounds' voices in the opposite direction.

High praise for the Grafton hounds that day came from an unlikely source: Higginson's good friend Julian Chamberlain, the very same man who had written to *Rider and Driver* back in January under his pseudonym "Lincoln" that these "chance bred" mutts could never show sport. Potts, who was with Chamberlain, Grafton Abbott, Jack Henderson from Clarke County, and Charles McEachran at the end of the run, reported that Chamberlain said, "that was by far the farthest and fastest run so far."

On Sunday the Great Hound Match was back on the front page headlined: "Higginson Is Fined for Trespass. . . . All of Piedmont Valley is agog over the arrest of A. Henry Higginson." Potts reported that Colonel Dulany had stepped in, afraid that "the good name of Loudoun County has been injured by the treatment of innocent strangers." Potts repeated what Higginson had told him—that Amos Payne had threatened to arrest the whole field. "This unfortunate affair has been the only unpleasant incident connected with the two weeks sport."

Sunday was a bye day for hunting, but there was a meeting of the judges to rule on the complaints filed by both Higginson and Smith. It was also a possibility that they could call an end to The Match then and there, which they did not do. They did, however, rule against Smith twice. First, that two weeks hunting meant that each side would have six, not seven, days hunting and second that Smith had no right to appoint a new judge to permanently replace Jim Maddux. Either Maddux would have to return as Smith's judge, or the remaining two judges, McEachran and Movius, would decide the outcome alone. The judges also reported that up to this point the Grafton hounds had runs totaling six hours and thirty-two minutes while the Middlesex hounds had run for four hours and fifty-eight minutes. Forty-two falls had been recorded and twelve horses, the equivalent of one box-car load from Massachusetts, had been permanently "put out of commission," not to mention scars and cuts from hitting walls, fences, ditches, and every other manner of obstacle.

Monday, November 13, was Middlesex's last day out. Do or die. The moon shone full that morning as riders set out for the meet on familiar territory, the Fred Farm north of Middleburg. Fifty-six riders turned out, including a few newcomers from Boston who had come for the last few days of hunting: James Roosevelt of Framingham, Massachusetts, as well as Mr. and Mrs. Byrd and Mr. and Mrs. Sturgess of Boston. Higginson announced that two coverts would be drawn, the first at Bald Hill woods. Cotesworth and his whips jogged the hounds down the road about a mile and turned into a field.

Just before reaching the woods all hell broke loose. The hounds dashed away without their huntsman and people began to yell.

"A fox!"

"Look! Look there!"

"Just there by the wall!"

Half the pack ran, heads up, sight-hunting a fox not three hundred yards away. Within seconds the hounds had rolled it over and killed it.

"Fair Kill!" half the people yelled, while the other half screamed "Bagged Fox!"

It must have been pandemonium. If the spectators hadn't been on horseback there probably would have been a fistfight. If it was indeed a fair kill, then The Match was over then and there; they could collect their money and the silver cup and go back home to New England. Dissenters threw cold water on the believers' elation, saying it was too easy, too soon, too quick. Higginson was the first to admit that "something was fishy."

Here's the gruesome part: It is customary to take a killed fox's "mask" (face) and his brush (tail) after a kill. Both were cut off the carcass and the rest was thrown to the hounds, for they did not recognize their kill as fair or foul. They got their reward. Everyone looked to the judges for their immediate decision. Unable to render one, they said they would make a ruling that evening; they needed more information. Higginson, having determined to hunt all day on his last day, ordered Cotesworth to take the hounds to the Bald Hill woods and continue with the planned hunt.

They found a fresh fox right away, the field viewed it running across Bald Hill, they had a nice run of around ten minutes, and jumped "some of the stiffest fences that they had encountered" according to Potts, including an uphill jump over a four-foot-eight-inch stone wall. Terry Dulany on Bachelor again wowed the crowd by jumping a wire-topped rail fence that had tied up the rest of the field. That particular fox went to ground under a rock ledge on Goose Creek. In the afternoon there were fresh horses waiting at Mountsville and they continued to Mr. Harrison's "Utopia" farm where they found again. But a pall must have hung over the day. Potts wrote in the next issue, "to put it mildly the most intense feeling prevailed throughout the day."

Morley Davis got to the bottom of the case of the pet fox: come to find out, a man named Hall had bought a pet fox from a farmer named McCauley, who had had the poor thing since May, had raised it by hand and sold it to Hall that morning for $4.50. Hall had been out hunting that day and watched the kill, but he never said a word. Morley Davis, after asking around the neighborhood, learned of the purchase and questioned Hall. Hall said that the fox had "broken loose" just before the hunt began. "It is most unfortunate that this unpleasant circumstance should have occurred during the most important hound match that has ever taken place," Potts writes. He was, as everyone must have been, appalled at the behavior of a foolish spoil-sport. Whether the man had intended to play a nasty practical joke or had sincerely wanted the Middlesex hounds to win was never determined. It's not against the law, only against the rules, to release a bagged fox. Late Monday night the judges ruled that the poor creature was a "turn-out"—shaken from a bag.

On Tuesday, November 14, there appeared a letter to the editors of the *Times-Dispatch* from a Mr. C. W. White of Warrenton. Keep in mind that Potts's reports from the field did not appear in the newspapers until the day after the events. Potts would probably have had to travel to Warrenton to send his reports by wire. The headline reads: "Higginson's Fine—A Club, not Mr. Amos Payne is responsible for it." Mr. White, a friend of Payne's, goes to great length—two full columns—to detail the circumstances by which Higginson came to be "arrested."

Evidently the whole of Loudoun and Fauquier Counties was not exactly in favor of The Great Hound Match taking place in their territory. Mr. White explains that when the decision was made back in the summer to hold The Match in Virginia a group of "seven or eight" farmers, neighbors who owned a total of about four thousand acres, had formed a "club . . . for their mutual protection." These men "were not willing that their fences and crops should be destroyed and their cattle stampeded and damaged . . . they insisted on their inherent right to say who should and should not come on their land . . . they were not willing to abandon their rights to the gentlemen and ladies of strenuous life, who for the time had invaded that section of the country." Notices had been written well before The Match began, placed in local Loudoun and Fauquier County papers, posted across their land, and sent as personal letters to all parties concerned including Messrs. Smith and Higginson.

The trespass must have happened on either November 6 or 8, when the Middlesex hounds were out chasing a fox across a newly sown field of wheat. Mr. Payne saw them go, saw the field follow and closed a gate to prevent them from returning. Payne asked someone in the field who was responsible for the trespass and was told that Mr. Higginson was in charge of the field that day. Payne made the complaint and a warrant was sworn against Higginson on Wednesday, November 8.

According to Mr. White, Higginson went to visit Mr. Payne the next day to apologize and to offer to pay any damages. Payne said he didn't want money, that he wanted Mr. Higginson's assurances that it wouldn't happen again and invited Higginson to meet with the other landowners, which he agreed to do the following day, Friday, at 1:00 p.m. The landowners assembled with their lawyer and waited, but Higginson didn't show. Friday was his day hunting and his hounds had holed a fox. His staff and terriers were digging it out. He couldn't possibly come. Furthermore, he would not be available later that day as there was to be a dinner that evening given by a local landowner and follower. Two men came in his place; "one had nothing to say, the other much." Higginson had appointed the talkative fellow, who was never named, as his "representative" and this man repeated the apologies, offers to pay, etc. Furthermore, he blamed Smith for Higginson's actions, "Smith of the Grafton hounds was wholly at fault; that he had led Mr. Higginson to believe that it was all right to go where he did." Again the members of the "club" said they didn't want money; they wanted to meet with Higginson, but that at this point they did have lawyers' fees and Higginson could cover them—around $100. A paper was drawn up and the "representative" and his silent friend drove off to give it to Mr. Higginson. The members of the "club" specified that they expected an answer by that evening or the next morning, Saturday, by 8:00 a.m. No answer came, so Higginson was arrested and taken before the magistrate in Warrenton.

Higginson lawyered up. First he agreed, then urged by his formerly agreeable "representative" refused, then agreed to pay $50. According to Mr. White it was never "contemplated that one cent of whatever would be paid would go to Mr. Payne . . . nor was Mr. Payne present at this consultation or consulted before it was concluded."

Two days later Potts writes the final chapter of the trespassing case: "The facts printed in the *Times-Dispatch* regarding the arrest of Mr. A. Henry Higginson by Mr. Amos Payne and the subsequent payment by Mr. Higginson of $50 to keep his friends from being arrested, were obtained from Mr. Higginson and his representative. The most intense feeling prevails here, and the magistrate before whom the case was to have been tried, called upon Colonel Dulany of Welbourne to explain that he had nothing to do with forcing Mr. Higginson to pay the $50."

The last day of The Match, Tuesday, November 14, was Grafton's, probably no accident—one reason that Smith had offered Higginson the first day may have been so that he could have the last. Potts's report is almost identical to Grafton's previous day, Sunday the 12th. Smith hunted the same thirteen hounds—six and a half couple—he'd been hunting every other day for the last two weeks. He'd only made two substitutions. Sinner was still his lead hound.

The Grafton pack set out from Oakley under a waxing gibbous moon illuminating snow on the mountaintops to the west where Orion, the Pleiades, and Taurus were setting. Snow on the mountains, to the old-timers in the crowd, forebode poor scent. They reached Miss Mounts farm at 7:30 and the hounds were uncoupled at 7:40. Sinner jumped a fox almost immediately near Steptoe Hill and his mates "harked to the line." Then they jumped two more—the same three foxes, the same fox conspiracy, that had dogged the hounds on Saturday. Sinner stuck to the original line. Smith's little whistle sounded "gone away" to gather stragglers and off they went on a two-hour chase, the longest, the fastest, the best of The Match. They flew over Goose Creek Hill, through "Utopia" and the Harrison estate, literally running away from the riders, disappearing across Chancellor's farm. Again the hounds had run away from the field. Smith took a "nasty fall," his horse landing on top of him in a ditch. "He was considerably shaken up," Potts writes, "but mounted his horse and followed hounds to the end." Again they ended up near Leesburg at Oatlands Plantation where the only two judges left for The Match, McEachran and Movius, recommended that they call it a day. Their decision would be discussed and given that very evening at Welbourne.

18

The Outcome

Tuesday, November 14, 1905
Welbourne, Upperville

EVENING FIRES AND GAS LAMPS WERE LIT IN EVERY ROOM OF WELBOURNE.
The house was full. In the west parlor, to the right of the foyer, where
Colonel Dulany's portrait hung above the fireplace, the judges were meeting—their verdict to be delivered—who knew when? The larger east parlor was filled with anxious foxhunters, many neighbors, curious townsfolk,
and Colonel Dulany's favorite foxhound, "Henry." Most foxhunters had
not bothered to change into their street clothes. Hovering in the room
there hung the unmistakable musk of horse, sweat, a little dried blood,
and damp wool. Two windows were cracked to let in some fresh air. Most
hands held a glass of the colonel's bourbon.

Books lined the west parlor walls, a piano in one corner, comfortable
chairs, warm carpets. Hal Movius and Charles McEachran were seated
and Jim Maddux, though he had not been out for the final two days of
hunting, had traveled from Warrenton to attend the last judges' meeting.
Allen Potts took notes. They had much to discuss. November 1 seemed
like months instead of weeks ago.

The judges had gotten to know one another quite well during The
Match. They'd been obligated not only to turn out to hunt, but to ride in
front with the Master every day. No one, except the judges, was expected
to hunt every single day of the two-week Match, which meant that they
had had to bring with them a string of horses that could withstand the
brutal pace and clear each formidable obstacle. On more than one day of
The Match at least one of the judges was present at the end when neither

Master was there. Maddux had had to drop out as a judge when his last horse, Wade, went lame on November 8. Smith had requested that Westmoreland Davis officially take his place, but that request had been overruled on Sunday the 12th. Davis had ridden one day as Smith's judge, but it had quickly become apparent that he was not able to keep up.

"Shall we begin?" Movius asked.

"Ready," Potts said.

"What an ending," Maddux said.

"You weren't there," McEachran said.

"I heard about it. Same three foxes jumped in the same field and run again all the way to Oatlands."

"It was a spectacular run," Movius said.

"Unbelievable," Maddux said. "I will say here and now, that Smith's American hounds are the fastest hounds in the universe. They can't be beat. They have no equal."

"I'll admit," McEachran said, "they are fast, very fast, but what good does it do to be that fast if the field can't keep up, if there are no riders at the end?"

"You were there. At the end. At Oatlands," Movius said. "Hell, even Chamberlain said that Saturday's run was the best in the Match."

"True, but Smith lost his own hounds. He claims they were in a gully and he couldn't hear them. Somehow Eastman found them and hunted them for him!"

"Eastman was with them all along," Maddux said.

"Again," Movius said. "You were not there."

"The Middlesex hounds ran extremely well on Monday," McEachran said. "We can't let the bagged fox distort our view. They ran true and hard and long."

"Their first run was seven minutes and the second was less than a quarter-mile," Maddux said. "Davis told me."

"The Middlesex put two foxes to ground on Monday," McEachran said.

"What do your notes say about Monday's run?" Movius asked Potts.

"You'll remember that we agreed last night not to include yesterday's hunt in the official record," Potts said.

There was an extended silence in the room. The fire crackled. Unbelievably, a fox called outside, in a field below a waning gibbous moon. A horse whinnied.

"The foxes won," Maddux said.

"Look," Movius said. "We need to bring this thing to a close. The running rules say that we must choose one or the other. Right, Potts?"

Potts looked back in his notes at the Running Rules and read aloud: "'The judges must render a decision, giving the match to one pack or the other.'"

"Shall we vote then?" Movius asked.

———

"Shhhhhh," Mrs. Pierce commanded. "Everyone. Please. Quiet down."

It had been two hours since the judges had sequestered themselves in the west parlor. In the meantime plenty of peanuts and bourbon had been consumed.

"I don't even care what they say," one man said. "This has been one hell of a fortnight."

"To The Match," someone called raising his glass, a chance for the room to drink again.

Harry Worcester Smith blew his whistle. The room quieted down.

Hal Movius stepped forward to read the results.

"We award the match and the stake together with the Townsend Cup to the Grafton Pack, which in our opinion, has done the best work with the object of killing the fox in view."

19

And Then *They* Came

1905–2015

THE FOXES WON. THEY OUTSMARTED, OUTRAN, OUTRAGED, AND OUTRIGHT outclassed the foxhounds and the foxhunters that November one hundred and ten years ago. The unstoppable in pursuit of the uncatchable. If one, just one, had let himself be legitimately killed by either the Middlesex or the Grafton hounds, so much of history would have changed. That martyred fox would have either crowned the English hound as *the* foxhound of the universe, or made it clear *once and for all* that there *is* an American foxhound and that it rules America.

Since no civic-minded fox stepped forward, and since the decision of the judges was in the end somewhat subjective, the question—which is better for America, the American or the English foxhound?—has never really been answered. "This decision settles, in a way at least," Allen Potts writes in the *Times-Dispatch*, Wednesday, November 15, "the much discussed question of superiority of relative merit of native and imported foxhounds in this country, but it is only fair to say that while the Grafton American hounds won the match, the Middlesex pack, of which Mr. A. Henry Higginson is master, furnished excellent sport in the Piedmont Valley during the trials." The fair thing to say is that life isn't fair and sport rarely is either.

The town of Middleburg won. Almost immediately Middleburg's fortunes began to rise. No longer would it be a forgotten creek-crossed, dirt-roaded, don't-blink-or-you'll-miss-it backwater. Were you on the train from The Plains back to Washington and on to New York, Boston, and Worcester, you probably would have overheard more than one conversation about real estate in Middleburg. Sure there was much bantering and loads of indignation about Higginson's arrest and the bagged fox and Smith's brazen brashness, those unbelievable horses and that amazing hound named Sinner, but the gist of the conversations was undoubtedly what a blast the whole thing had been and now they had to go back to New England where the scent would be buried under a foot or two of snow until April.

"This morning the Middlesex Hunt party left for Massachusetts with thirty-five horses, fifty hounds, and a great retinue of hunt and personal servants," Allen Potts writes the day after The Match ended. "During the trials the Middlesex Hunt purchased fifteen hunters from the farmers over whose land they rode and these have been shipped North with the rest of the string." Higginson, Mrs. Abbott, Mrs. Pierce, Julian Chamberlain, Leonard Ahl, Mrs. Perkins, Miss Byrd, Dr. Charles McEachran, and Hal Movius were on the train. "Mr. Higginson was in no way depressed by the decision of the judges." His popularity during The Match was evident. "It was learned that some thirty-five land owners around Middleburg sent Mr. Higginson a written request to take over that hunting section and to establish his pack there." But before Mr. Higginson could leave town, Courtland Smith, Harry's brother, attached a $78.00 lien against Higginson's horses. Courtland Smith also sued Mrs. Pierce for the price of Champion, the horse that she'd bought from him on Sunday and returned on Thursday, claiming the horse was lame due to a torn tendon he'd received while jumping a rail fence during the second week of The Match. "The Middlesex crowd say they have had more suits brought against them during their two weeks stay in Virginia than all the rest of their lives," Potts writes.

After The Match Smith stuck around Upperville through Thanksgiving. There was of course a grand "Sportsman's Dinner" in the Grafton pack's honor given by J. William Yates, "a grand old sportsman" who lived in Markham, a town on the eastern edge of the Blue Ridge Mountains in what was then, and is still known, as Virginia's "Free State" because of its lawless bootlegging history. Markham lies about twelve miles southwest of Upperville and was hard to reach in 1905 given the deplorable conditions of the roads. This is the country described in "Old Whitey's Run," a story by Albin S. Payne, a Fauquier County country doctor who wrote under the pseudonym "Nicholas Spicer" in the mid-1800s. Old

Whitey was the white-tailed fox who deceived the Free State's foxhunters for nearly two years before they gathered from all corners of northern Virginia to run him down in the kind of "gallus" foxhunting that Harry Worcester Smith admired and Alexander Henry Higginson deplored.[1]

"So as to be on time [for the dinner], not knowing just how bad the road was to Markham I had started around 9 o'clock and so had a glorious appetite," Smith writes in a letter to the *Loudoun Fauquier Magazine*, April 14, 1933, in which he describes the dinner at Mr. Yates's home "high up in the mountains." The guests arrived at 4:00 p.m., carrying with them poultry, game, and fish they had killed and caught for the feast, "and in addition their good wives aided with jellies, ketchups, etc." Black bean soup "so thick that the lemon floated proudly on top" was the first course, followed by fried trout with salt pork, "and as there were over thirty people about the table, the catch that was needed to supply such a gathering for first and second helpings can be imagined." For the main course there was quail, chicken, "five great turkeys," suckling pig, gray squirrel, "and the most delicious pickled sliced green tomatoes that I ever tasted." Dessert was "mince pies, apple pies, custard pies, doughnuts and cheese." The men must have stood to honor Harry Worcester Smith and his hounds. Possibly a toast: "To the Americans! To the American Master!" No doubt after a dinner like that he stayed a day or two with Mr. Yates. In fact, he stayed at the Dulanys' through Thanksgiving, which is still a big foxhunting day in Virginia. Oakley and Welbourne must have been uncommonly quiet when Harry Worcester Smith left.

It took a couple of years, six in fact, for the real estate around Upperville to start moving. The first invader to actually purchase land was Brigadier General James A. Buchanan, who retired from the army in 1906 after serving in Puerto Rico and the Philippines. In 1912 Buchanan bought Ayrshire outside Upperville.[2] Harry Worcester Smith, writing in his memoirs, laid out the cost of coming to Virginia: "The sensible sportsman who wants to locate in Virginia should have large enough income so that he can expend from five to forty or fifty thousand dollars a year on his Southern venture, exclusive of his subscriptions to hunts, living and stable. It must have cost General Buchanan . . . near Upperville, at least twenty or thirty thousand a year to keep up his splendid mansion, where he dispensed generous hospitality, and pursued his breeding operations."

In 1914 the cotton broker Edward M. Weld bought "North Wales," former home of six generations of Allasons near Leesburg who were granted the property by Lady Catherine Culpepper Fairfax. Weld spent $1.5 million (in 1905 dollars) for the 1,100-acre property, "stretched [the 1773 house] to seventy-two rooms, added a racing stable of forty stalls and a six furlong covered track, filled the cellars with $50,000 worth of liquors, and went broke."[3]

Originally home of the FFVs—First Families of Virginia—by 1930 the Piedmont was soon home to the Chicago, Detroit, Boston, and New York's finest, or wealthiest anyway. *Fortune* ran an article titled "Jericho Road" in November 1930, just over a year after the stock market crashed. Edward Henry "Ned" Harriman, the rags-to-riches railroad man from Long Island, was one of the founders of the Orange County hunt in New York, which had moved its winter quarters to The Plains. After The Match, Harriman paid to have the road between Middleburg and The Plains macadamized, which is why it is still known as the (2nd) "Jericho Road." The *Fortune* article about the Northern Invasion is written with tongue firmly in cheek; the editors must have felt that sufficient time had passed to satirize what had become of the once quiet, nearly forgotten, place. "Here the fledgling millionaires are completely exonerated from all affectations about work."[4] As the comic poet Ogden Nash (1902–1971) once said, "The Virginians from Virginia have to ride automobiles because the Virginians from Long Island are the only ones who can afford to ride horses."

Harry Worcester Smith made it crystal clear to the *Fortune* reporter: "I was the first outsider from the north" to come to Virginia to hunt. "The match and its publicity really made Virginia." *Fortune* drops names: "Here hunt the Walter Wests of St. Louis, the racing Zieglers, Raymond Belmont, Charley Sabins, Edith Cummings of Chicago, the Henry Whitfields, the Arthur Whites, and the famous horse dealers Otto Furr and Louis Leith"—and on and on and on. The famous followed the rich. George Patton hunted with the Piedmont, about which Harry Worcester Smith had this to say in an April 6, 1945, interview with the *Worcester*

Telegram: "he [Patton] rode hard with us and was able to keep up with us two-thirds of the way."

Immediately after The Match, in the spring and summer of 1906, both Smith and Higginson were making plans to come back to Virginia to hunt. Smith moved ahead with his dream of making the Piedmont "the fox-hunting center of America." The Piedmont Hunt voted early that year to split into East and West countries, both under the larger Piedmont Hunt umbrella, with Smith master of the East—around Middleburg—and Dick Dulany (Rozier's cousin) Master of the West around Upperville. Their plan was published in *The Sportsman's Review* 30 (1906) with the expressed intent to open the country to all Masters of Foxhounds in the United States, "not as an exclusive club, but as a sportsman's club in the broadest sense of the word." As usual, Smith didn't dream small. But his egalitarian vision of fox-hunting for all was blinded before it could see; he was driven out of Virginia by the beginnings of the everlasting hunt-country turf wars.

Smith blames John R. "Jack" Townsend. Townsend was Master of the Orange County (New York) Hunt, which had set up its winter headquarters in The Plains, the same folks whose path had crossed Smith's while he was hunting south of the Ashby Gap Turnpike during The Match. After The Match, according to Smith, Mr. Townsend "deliberately set about to steal the Middleburg country away from the Piedmont."[5] This was the same country that Smith had been given charge of in his joint Piedmont Mastership. "He [Townsend] went to Middleburg, leased the Fred farm, started a new hunt which he called the Middleburg Hunt, which as told in A. Henry Higginson's *The Hunts of the United States and Canada* published in 1908, 'was nothing more or less than an offshoot of the Orange County.'" *The Hunts of the United States and Canada*, coauthored by Higginson's friend Julian Chamberlain, describes "a good deal of trouble between Mr. Harry W. Smith and Mr. John R. Townsend" during the spring of 1906: "Mr. Townsend eventually got the better of the dispute."[6] Higginson must have had something to do with the dispute since "in the spring of 1906 Mr. Higginson received an invitation from the Masters of both the Piedmont and the Loudoun Hunts to take three days of their respective countries for the following season."[7] Higginson was Master at Loudoun from 1906 to 1909 with Bob Cotesworth serving as his huntsman the first season, but resigning the next when Higginson began hunting his own hounds.

After one of those seasons in Middleburg, Higginson found himself sitting next to Smith's friend Thomas Hitchcock, Master of Meadow Brook on Long Island and an American hound man, on the train back home to New England. "You mark my words, you'll change just as I did," Hitchcock told Higginson, trying to convince him that someday Higginson too would be an American hound man.[8] Though that day never came, in 1919 "keeping abreast of current developments in Britain," Higginson elected to "introduce Welsh strains into his pack, by importing a number of hounds from Sir Edward Curre's at Itton Court" to counteract the Belvoir influence on his English hounds.[9]

Smith resigned his Mastership of the Piedmont in the fall of 1906. "It really seemed, when I wrote my letter of resignation to Dick Dulany," Smith writes in his memoirs, "that I was putting to one side the greatest aim of my life in sport which for a number of years I had been striving unceasingly to attain—the Mastership of a pack of hounds in the best hunting country in America, so the bitterness in my heart can well be appreciated."[10]

Two very good things came of this first skirmish in the hunt turf wars: first, the Jericho Turnpike was paved and second, Harry Worcester Smith "went to work to found the Masters of Foxhounds Association."[11] Prior to The Match Smith and the Dulanys had drawn a careful map of the Piedmont country, had published it in *Rider and Driver* in October 1905, and had submitted it to the National Steeplechase and Hunt Association, which held jurisdiction over hunts in the United States at the time. Smith wrote to the NSHA to ask that they make a ruling on Middleburg's encroachment on Piedmont's territory. Politics ensued; officers of the NSHA were also officers of Orange County Hunt, and the NSHA declined to rule. So Smith did what he usually did, he started a new association "which would take jurisdiction of the sport, exist for that purpose alone, and be controlled by the Masters themselves, not by members of the Jockey Club or the National Steeplechase and Hunt Association."[12] Of all the things Harry Worcester Smith did throughout his long life, the founding of the MFHA is universally recognized as the most important.

Smith served as president of the MFHA for three years before he was, according to Smith, usurped again by Alexander Henry Higginson in 1916. Higginson was president for the next seventeen years and was subsequently appointed honorary vice president for life when he moved to England permanently. According to Smith, upon being appointed president, Higginson redesigned the MFHA seal, which is still in use today, featuring Bob Cotesworth "holding a biscuit for a heavy hound with enough lumber to pull a dray, and knuckled over on the knees," — clearly an English hound.

Smith was Master of Loudoun, after Higginson, from 1909 to 1912, and then he packed up his hounds, his horses, his new car, his tack and his whistle, hired five African American hunt servants—Norman Brooks, Dolph Wheeler, Sam Webster, Wiley Thrash, and Joe Thomas—and went to Ireland to become the first American Master of a hunt in the British Isles—the Westmeath in Ireland 1912–1913. He must have felt compelled to return to the Old Country to show them exactly how it was done. Imagine the spectacle when Smith and his entourage arrived in Ireland. The hounds were put into quarantine, but soon enough, when it stopped raining, they went hunting. "In 1912 Harry Smith took on the mastership of Westmeath in Ireland," Higginson writes in *An Old Sportsman's Memories, 1876–1951.* "There are today some English and Irish sportsmen and women who may remember the way *that* American invasion was conducted. I need say no more."[13]

It is safe to say that Harry Worcester Smith and Alexander Henry Higginson hated one another for the rest of their lives. Their tit-for-tat history of bickering bordered on childish and can be read in both men's published and unpublished manuscripts. "I must admit," Higginson writes in 1951, "that the unpleasant taste which was left in my mouth after the match with regard to *one individual* (his italics), has never worn off, I am thankful to say that it is not predominant in my memory, in fact it is almost forgotten." Right. This was written six years after Harry Worcester Smith's death. In 1939, after reading a comment by Higginson in a British publication, Smith writes that Higginson "is still smarting over his defeat in Virginia, for since that time he has done nothing but throw mud at the American hounds, and now has begun to include the Master, Huntsman and Whippers-in."[14]

"Looking back at the incidents with which those two weeks in the fall of 1905 were crowded," Higginson writes in *Try Back*, his 1931 memoir, "it seems to me that Mr. Smith and I both took the outcome of the match too seriously. We were both young and perhaps over-enthusiastic, and I think we both felt that the reputation of American and English hounds depended on the outcome of the match, whereas in reality if we had only known something more about foxhunting we might have realized that both sorts of hounds have their uses and are excellent under certain conditions of scent and country." Alexander Henry Higginson may have been a young man in 1905—he was twenty-nine—but Harry Worcester Smith turned forty-one November 6, 1905. He was twelve years older than Higginson and had been foxhunting for at least that long before The Match. "I was naturally disappointed at the ultimate decision of the judges," Higginson continues, "I made no comments at the time nor have I since."[15] No, but he never stopped writing about it. He fictionalized The Match in *The Perfect Follower* (London: Collins) as late as 1944.

Higginson's Middlesex stable burned in 1914, destroying twenty-two of his twenty-six horses, "twenty-two glowing spots in the ashes."[16] His father, Henry Lee Higginson, said, "Too bad Sonny, don't worry, it's all right . . . just go ahead and get the best lot of hunters you can find in the country and send the bill to me."[17] Later, when a similar fire took his barn in Lake Champlain, he was not insured "and this time I had no father to come and help me out of my trouble."[18] His second wife, Jeanne Calducci, a showgirl from New York who had starred in musical comedies including "Winsome Winnie" at the New York Casino, died in 1925 of tuberculosis, complications from the 1918 influenza epidemic. Higginson's father, Henry Lee Higginson, died in 1919. Before he died, he and Ida traveled back to Aldie, where he had been wounded in the war. There he met a farmer who knew the story of the battle and had known of Major Higginson's having been wounded. In 1902 Henry Lee Higginson petitioned the state of Massachusetts to begin licensing automobiles, which led to the creation of the modern license plate. He also took part in the first transcontinental telephone conversation with Alexander Graham Bell,

Thomas Watson, Theodore Vail, and Woodrow Wilson. Henry Lee Higginson's time with the Boston Symphony Orchestra ended lamentably and unsatisfactorily during the First World War when his German-born music director, Karl Muck, was interned as an enemy alien and Higginson obstinately refused to add the Star Spangled Banner to the orchestra's list of highlighted pieces. "His life was one of service to others," Alexander Henry Higginson writes about his father in *An Old Sportsman's Memories*, "whereas I am afraid that mine has been devoted to the pursuit of happiness, with little thought for those about me, except my immediate family."

When the Great War came Alexander Henry Higginson's main problem was "the quality of hounds which were available for importation."[19] Recognizing that "hunting men had been among the first to answer the call to arms," Higginson presented a toast at a dinner in New York given for Charles McNeill, former MFH of Grafton (England) and North Cotswold, who had come over to buy horses for the British army: "To the hunting men of England, Masters of Hounds, followers in the field, and Hunt servants, good sportsmen all of them who are now at the front, fighting for their country and their King, and may they soon come home victorious with their colors flying to carry on the sport which has made such gallant soldiers."[20] Higginson's second whipper-in, George Thorne, returned to England in 1916 and died soon afterward in France. Higginson sold his Middlesex pack in 1919.

Smith writes in the spring of 1919 about his World War I impressions: "I stood on the hill at Monticello, the very day the Germans were making their tremendous drive, wondering if Hun efficiency was to rule the world . . . the sportsmen of England and America and the French soldiers held them . . . it was a pleasure to stand there just a year later and know that those people who loved the cry of the hounds in the woodland, the scarlet jacket over water, the green turf of the race course, the jumping of a trout to a fly, the cry of 'fore' on the golf links, the 'play ball' on the diamond, the flying wedge on the football field and above all Fair Play, had won."[21]

In 1926 Higginson married his third wife, Mary Newcomb, a London stage actress, and in 1931 they moved to England permanently. Beginning in 1929 he began writing and publishing foxhunting anthologies; short fictional stories; biographies of famous foxhunters and British and

American sporting authors; books on the theory and practice of foxhunting; and two autobiographies. He also compiled and edited the first five volumes of the MFHA *Foxhound Kennel Stud Book*. Higginson was Master of the South Dorset and Cattistock Hunt, West Dorset, England. He lived his last years in Stinson House, Dorchester, Dorset, where he bred English foxhounds, including S. Dorset "'Salesman'44, that most influential of modern sires."[22]

Smith sold his pack of American hounds in 1916. His home, Lordvale, burned to the ground early Friday morning, April 14, 1940. His wife Mildred's family home Mariemont was destroyed in the great hurricane of 1944. Mildred Crompton Smith was the first woman in Worcester to get her driver's license. Harry and Mildred's children and grandchildren carried the dominant horse-loving gene; Harry's son Crompton became a great horseman and his grandson Tommy, riding his $2,000 horse, "Jay Trump," was the first American jockey ever to win the English Grand National Steeplechase on an American horse. His granddaughter Kitty Smith is a well-known Piedmont horsewoman.

Smith was larger than life, greater than the sum of his parts. Reading about his life, usually written by himself, is like watching or reading "Forest Gump"—someone famous is always cropping up. For instance he proudly chauffeured Teddy Roosevelt around Worcester, not once but twice, in 1905 and 1914, in a four-in-hand rig. In 1916 he jumped 7'2" on Success, one of his string of hunters in The Match. He received this Valentine Day's card from an admirer in Aiken, South Carolina:

> "Oh, Harry Smith, Oh, Harry Smith,
>   You're as cold as you can be;
>   You smile at other ladies,
>   But you never look at me.
> I stand and watch you riding by
>   In your socks and tie of red,
> With your twinkling eyes and curly hair,
>   You've turned my foolish head."[23]

"Let it be said that Harry Worcester Smith suffers from no inferiority complex. Superior men never do."[24]

In the 1920s and 1930s Smith spent his middle age researching and writing about the life of Edward Troye, arguably the greatest American equine portraitist of the nineteenth century. "Beginning with a match race in October, 1832, Edward Troye followed the racing circuit where he met, visited, and stayed with the most wealthy and influential individuals in the aristocratic south before and after the Civil War."[25] Troye painted America's foundation bloodstock before photography was invented; he was a traveling artist who lived with and was respected by the greatest equine breeders and racing men of the time. American Eclipse, Lexington, Sir Archy, Medley, Trifle, Tranby, Kentucky, Reel, Glencoe, Roebuck, Asteroid, and Australian are among the hundreds of important American mares and stallions Troye painted. Many of his paintings were lost, hidden, misplaced, and forgotten after the Civil War and Harry Worcester Smith made it his mission to find and restore them. "For the Sake of Sport in America," Smith spent the better part of three decades driving through Virginia, Kentucky, Tennessee, Alabama, and North and South Carolina in search of Troye's work. He saw "not only the beauty and precision of Troye's equine art, but the importance of Troye's early documentation of America's foundation thoroughbred bloodstock."[26] The culmination of his discovery, resurrection, and acquisition—he bought many works for himself and other patrons—was the first gallery exhibition of Troye's work at the Newhouse Galleries in New York City on November 15 to 26, 1938. "With Smith's help, Troye came down from mantelpieces, out of parlors, entries and bedrooms, into galleries, collections and museum."[27]

Smith sold his beloved sporting library on December 10, 1931, possibly due to the stock-market crash, including: *Hunting Reminiscences* by Charles J. Apperley (1843); *Thoughts on Hunting* by Peter Beckford with colored plates by G. Denholm Armour signed by the artist; an original copy of the proclamation of Oliver Cromwell prohibiting horse racing for six months in 1654—"in perfect condition bound in a full blue morocco folder (*Worcester Evening Gazette*, Thursday, May 20, 1948); *Cavelarice* or *English Horsemen* by Gervase Markham, London 1617; John Masefield's "Reynard the Fox" signed by the author and illustrator; as well as several Wedgewood Cameo Medallions of Horses designed by George Stubbs. The sale catalogue's introduction reads: "My wish is that my drawings, my prints, my curiosities, my Books—in a word these things of art which have been the joy of my life—shall not be consigned to the cold tomb of a museum, and subjected to the stupid glance of a careless passerby; but I require that they shall all be dispersed under the hammer of the Auctioneer, so that the pleasure which the acquiring of each one of them has given me shall be given again, in each case, to some inheritor of my own tastes."[28] Higginson went to the sale. Across the top of his copy of the catalogue, held in the London Library's Alexander Henry Higginson collection, Higginson jotted, "A very disappointing lot of books, many in bad condition and many being inaccurately described." He then adds, paradoxically, "The prices are far below their value, there are some good items . . . disappointing sale."[29] There was only one book by Alexander Henry Higginson in the Harry Worcester Smith sale. By contrast, "upon Mr. Higginson's death in 1958, his library contained virtually everything published on foxhunting in the British Isles, but nothing on American foxhunting."[30] And no books by Harry Worcester Smith.

"Ever since the beginning, hunting men have found a need to justify their sport and endow it with a higher purpose," Alexander Henry Higginson writes in *An Old Sportsman's Memories*. Hunting was once the "high point of breeding and courage," he muses—"I would rather end my days peacefully in England . . . perhaps 'go to ground' in the churchyard at Claybrooke, Leicestershire, whence the first Higginson set sail for the New World in 1629."[31]

Late in life Harry Worcester Smith mused the age-old question, "Who will finish or continue my accumulation of Thought, Feeling and Art?" He wrote on the front of an envelope with a return address—Harry Worcester Smith, Nimrod Hall, The Plains, Virginia—as if he intended to mail it to the universe and expected a reply.[32]

On November 28, 2013, a three-year-old American foxhound named G. C. H. Kiarry's Pandora's Box (AKA "Jewel"), won Best in Show out of two thousand entries at the US National Dog Show. Is Jewel the crowning glory of Harry Worcester Smith's efforts to have the American foxhound recognized as a separate and equal breed of hound dog?

To be sure, the debate still rages among hound men, in America at least. Twice, in 1989 and 1991, The Match was reenacted in Middleburg. The first was snowed out, the second was won by the Midland Fox Hounds under the legendary Benjamin H. Hardaway III and his English/American *crossbred* foxhounds.

Glossary of Foxhunting Terms

(From *Riding to Hounds in America; an Introduction for Foxhunters* by William P. Wadsworth, MFH. Middleburg, VA: *The Chronicle of the Horse*, 1987.)

AWAY—A fox has "gone away" when he has left covert. Hounds are "away" when they have left covert on the line of a fox.

BABBLE—To give tongue on scent other than a fox, on no scent at all, or on a scent too faint to follow.

BLANK—To draw blank is to fail to find a fox.

BRUSH—A fox's tail is always called a brush.

BUTTON—To receive, or be awarded the button is to be given the right to wear the hunt buttons and colors.

BYE—A bye day is a hunting day not scheduled on the fixture card. An extra dividend.

CAP—1. (n) The safe headgear for foxhunters. 2. (v or n) To "pass the hat" among the field. Visitors may be "capped" or asked to pay a "capping fee." A hunt may have a "cap" for some particular purpose, such as paneling, charity, etc.

CAST—1. (n) A planned move in searching for a lost line (trail). 2. (v) To make a cast. Hounds may cast themselves, or the huntsman may cast them.

CHECK—1. (n) An interruption of the run caused by hounds losing the line. 2. (v) Hounds check when they lose the line temporarily.

COLORS—1. (n) The distinctive colors that distinguish the uniform of one hunt from another. Usually a distinctive color of collar on a scarlet coat. (Some hunts have coats other than scarlet.) 2. (v) To be awarded or given the colors is to be given the right to wear them and the hunt button.

COUPLE—1. (n) Two hounds (any sex), for convenience in counting. 2. (n) a device for keeping two hounds attached to each other for convenience in control or training. 3. (v) To attach two hounds together by use of couples.

COVERT—(pronounced cover) A patch of woods or brush where a fox might be found.

CROP—The stiff portion of a hunting whip, to which the thong is attached. (Also incorrectly applied to the whole whip, i.e., crop, thong, and lash.)

CRY—(n) The sound given by hounds when hunting, e.g., "The pack, in full cry."

CUB—A young fox.

CUBHUNTING—Early hunting before the formal season. Hounds are encouraged to stay in covert, foxes that go away being permitted to do so in peace if practical. This gets cubs in the habit of running straight, rather than circling in covert.

DOUBLE BACK—A fox that returns to covert after having left it is said to double back.

DRAW—1. (v) To search for a fox in a certain area, e.g., "To draw a covert." 2. (n) The act of drawing, e.g., "Thorny Wood is a difficult draw." 3. (v) To select and separate a hound or group of hounds in kennels for a particular purpose, e.g., "Please draw out Bluebell's last year's litter, so I can show them to Mr. . . ."

DRIVE—The urge to get forward well with the line, e.g., "That hound has drive."

DWELL—To hunt without getting forward. A hound that lacks drive is apt to dwell.

EARTH—Any place where a fox goes to ground for protection, but usually a place where foxes live regularly—a fox den.

ENTER—A hound is "entered" when he is first regularly used for hunting. "This year's entry" are the hounds entered or to be entered this season.

FEATHER—A hound "feathers" when he indicates, by actions rather than by voice, that he is on a line or near it. The stern is waved, and activity is concentrated and intensified.

FIELD—The group of people riding to hounds, excluding the MFH and staff.

FIELD MASTER—The person designated by the MFH to control the field.

FIXTURE—The time and place of the meet, or assembly of the hunt. A fixture card is a card sent out to list the fixtures for a given period.

GROUND—"To go to ground." To take shelter (usually underground), e.g., "The fox went to ground in the main earth east of the swamp."

HEAD—(v) To head a fox is to cause it to turn from its planned direction of travel. This usually causes a check, and is not recommended.

HEEL—(adv) Backward. Hounds following the line the wrong way are running "heel" (also called "counter").

HOLD HARD—"Stop, please." If used twice to the same individual, it probably means "Stop, please, damn you."

HONOR—A hound "honors" when he gives tongue on a line that another hound has been hunting.

HUNTING WHIP—The assembly of crop, thong, and lash is known as a hunting whip, incorrectly as a crop or hunting crop.

HUNTSMAN—The man who controls hounds in the field.

LARK—To jump fences unnecessarily when hounds are not running, or on non-hunting days. (Annoys landowners. Not recommended.)

LASH—The short piece of cord (occasionally leather) attached to the end of the whip thong away from the crop. Sometimes improperly applied to both thong and lash as a unit.

LIFT—To carry hounds forward. Usually implies that hounds were hunting when lifted. (Risky, but sometimes advisable. Don't crab the huntsman unless he does it often.)

LINE—The trail of the fox.

LITTER—A group of young born of the same mother at the same time. In foxhunting applies to whelps (puppies) or cubs. Equally correct when applied to kittens or pigs.

MARK—(To ground) A hound "marks" when he indicates that a fox has gone to ground. He stops at the earth, tries to dig his way in, and gives tongue in a way quite different from his hunting voice. Some hounds are better at marking than others.

MASTER—The MFH (Master of Fox Hounds). The person in command of the hunt in field and kennels.

MEET—The assembling of the hunt for a day's sport, e.g., "The meet tomorrow is at ..." or "Hounds meet tomorrow at ..."

NOSE—The ability of a hound to detect and interpret the scent.

OPEN—A hound is said to "open" when he first gives tongue on a line.

PAD—1. The foot of a fox. 2. The center cushion of a hound's foot.

PANEL—1. The portion of any jumpable fence between two posts. 2. A jumpable portion built into a wire fence.

POINT—1. The straight line distance made good in a run, e.g., "That was a six-mile point, but twelve miles as hounds ran." 2. The location to which a whipper-in is sent to watch for a fox to go away.

RATCATCHER—Informal hunting attire. Correct for cubbing.

RATE—A warning cry given to correct hounds. The words are less important than the intonation, e.g., "Back to him" or "Ware riot."

RIDE—(n) A lane cut through woods.

RIOT—Anything that hounds might hunt that they shouldn't.

RUN—(n) A period during which hounds are actually hunting on the line of a fox. (Usually implies a gallop for the field, as opposed to a "hunt in covert after a twisting fox.")

SCENT—The smell of a fox, and the physical and chemical phenomena by which the smell gets from the fox's footprints to the hound's nose. Scent can be good or bad, meaning easy to follow or difficult. It depends in general on weather.

SPEAK—To give tongue. (Usually of a single hound, e.g., "I heard old Homer open, and he spoke for some time before the others got to him.")

STAFF—The huntsman and whippers-in.

STERN—Tail of a hound.

THONG—The long flexible braided leather portion of a hunting whip joining the lash to the crop.

TONGUE—1. (n) Cry. A hound "gives tongue" when he proclaims with his voice that he is on a line. 2. (v) To give tongue.

VIEW—(v or n) See (or sight of) the fox.

VIEW HOLLOA—The cry given by a staff member on viewing a fox.

WALK—Puppies are "sent out at walk" in the summer and fall of their first year, preferably on farms where they learn about chickens, etc.

WARE—A caution (1) To riders, e.g., "Ware wire." (2) To hounds, e.g., "Ware riot." Usually pronounced "war." An abbreviation of beware.

WHELP—(n) A young puppy; (v) to bear puppies, e.g., "That hound was whelped 3/6/87."

WHIPPER-IN—A staff member who assists the huntsman in the control of hounds.

NOTES

Preface and Acknowledgments

1. Arthur Krystal, "The Age of Reason," *The New Yorker*, October 22, 2007, accessed October 21, 2014, www.newyorker.com/magazine/2007/10/22.

Chapter 1

1. J. Blan Van Urk, *The Story of American Foxhunting: From Challenge to Full Cry* (New York: Derrydale Press, ca. 1940–1941), 1:7.
2. Alexander Henry Higginson, *Try Back: A Huntsman's Reminiscences* (New York: Huntington Press, 1931), 15.
3. Barbara Schmidt, "Mark Twain Quotations, Newspaper Collections and Related Resources," accessed October 31, 2014, www.twainquotes .com/19351102.html.

Chapter 2

1. "Running Rules for the Grafton-Middlesex Foxhound Match Held in the Piedmont Valley, Virginia, November 1 to 15, 1905" are in Appendix A in Alexander Mackay-Smith's *The American Foxhound 1747–1967* (Millwood, VA: American Foxhound Club, 1968). Appendix B is the "Grafton-Middlesex Foxhound Match 1905 Official Minutes and Reports" submitted by Allen Potts each day of The Match.

Chapter 3

1. William M. Sloane, "Life of Napoleon Bonaparte," *Century Magazine* L, no. 5 (1895): 643.
2. Glenn Alexander Magee, *The Hegel Dictionary* (New York: The Continuum International Publishing Group, 2010), 262. Hegel is credited with the term "zeitgeist," based on the quoted phrase in Magee. Interestingly, "The Spirit of the Times" was also the name of the most popular sporting magazine in 1839. It was published in New York.
3. Lizzie J. Maggie Phillips invented the game in 1903; its first rendition was published in 1906.
4. Jackson Lears, *Rebirth of a Nation* (New York: HarperCollins, 2009), 284.

5. Joseph Horowitz, *Moral Fire; Musical Portraits from America's Fin-de-Siècle* (Berkeley: University of California Press, 2012), xii.

6. Horowitz, *Moral Fire*, 2.

7. Mim Eichler Rivas, *Beautiful Jim Key: The Lost History of a Horse and a Man Who Changed the World* (New York: HarperCollins, 2005), 41. (No wonder the good doctor, though on his third marriage when Jim was foaled, had no children of his own.)

8. William Kloss and Doreen Bolger, *Art in the White House: A Nation's Pride* (Washington, D.C.: The White House Historical Association in cooperation with the National Geographic Society, 1992), www.whitehouseresearch.org/assetbank-whha/action/viewAsset?id=134.

9. Walt Whitman, *Leaves of Grass* (Philadelphia: David McKay [ca. 1900], Bartleby.com, accessed May 16, 2014, http://www.bartleby.com/142/.

10. Abraham Pais, *Neils Bohr's Times: In Physics, Philosophy, and Polity* (Oxford: Clarendon Press, 1991), 3.

11. Abraham Pais, *Subtle Is the Lord: The Science and the Life of Albert Einstein* (Oxford: Oxford University Press, 1982), 44.

12. "Albert Einstein," A&E Network, accessed March 6, 2014, www.history.com/topics/albert-einstein/videos#beyond-the-big-bang-albert-einstein.

13. Pais, *Subtle Is the Lord*, 47.

14. Pais, *Neils Bohr's Times*, 3.

15. "Dr. Albert Einstein Dies in Sleep at 76; World Mourns Loss of Great Scientist," *New York Times*, April 19, 1955, accessed March 6, 2014, www.nytimes.com/learning/general/onthisday/bday/0314.html. (This article was written the day after Einstein's death, ten days after the day I was born. Evidently no one asked a woman.)

16. Pais, *Subtle Is the Lord*, 14. (Einstein's Foreword to a 1931 reprint of Newton's *Opticks*. Einstein, the philosopher, writes in the same essay: "Fortunate Newton, happy childhood of science.")

17. Stanley Hoffman, introduction to *Consciousness and Society*, by H. Stuart Hughes (New Brunswick, NJ: Transaction, 2008), xiv.

18. William James, "Pragmatism: A New Name for Some Old Ways of Thinking," in *Writings 1902–1910*. (New York: Literary Classics of the United States, Inc., 1987), 491.

19. William James, "Pragmatism," 508.

20. William James admitted that nitrous oxide "made me understand better than ever before both the strength and the weakness of Hegel's philosophy," accessed June 25, 2014, www.uky.edu/~eushe2/Pajares/jnitrous.html.

21. William James, "The Varieties of Religious Experience: A Study in Human Nature," in *Writings 1902–1910* (New York: Literary Classics of the United States, Inc., 1987), 11.

22. George Santayana, *Character & Opinion in the United States: With Reminiscences of William James and Josiah Royce and Academic Life in America* (New York: Charles Scribner's Sons, 1922), 5.

23. Horowitz, *Moral Fire*, 225.

24. William James, "Some Problems of Philosophy," in *Writings 1902–1910*, 987.

25. Henry James, "Religion and Neurology," in *Writings*, 21.

26. Philip Horne, "James, Henry (1843–1916)," *Oxford Dictionary of National Biography*, accessed March 7, 2014, www.oxforddnb.com/view/article/34150.

27. Bertrand Russell, *A History of Western Philosophy* (New York: Simon & Schuster, 1945), 811. (Comparing William to Henry, Russell writes, "He [William] refused altogether to follow his brother Henry into fastidious snobbishness.")

Chapter 4

1. It is not clear whether Mr. Higginson followed the first day on horseback or by buggy. The *Richmond Times-Dispatch* reported that Higginson stated in the October 31 meeting of Masters and Judges that he would not ride on the first day. On November 2, when the first day's run hit the papers, the same paper reported that Mr. Higginson "followed" but it did not say whether he was on horseback or in a buggy.

Chapter 5

1. Joseph E. Woods, *The Worcester County West Agricultural Society: A Brief History of the Barre Cattle Shows* (Worcester, MA: The Shelly Print, 1914), 5–6.

2. Josephine McCurdy Caroline Lord Smith, *A Sketch of Mrs. C. W. Smith's Life Written by Herself, 1909*, self-published, held at the American Antiquarian Society, Worcester, MA, 10.

3. Robert Morris Washburn, *The Smith's Barn: A Child's History of the West Side, Worcester 1880–1923* (Worcester MA: Exclusive distributors, Davis & Banister, 1923), 9–11.

4. Ibid.

5. Ibid., 64.

6. Ibid., 26.

7. Ibid., 11.

8. Held in Worcester Polytechnic Institute archives.

9. Herbert Foster Taylor, *Seventy Years of the Worcester Polytechnic Institute* (Worcester, MA: Worcester Polytechnic Institute), 161–62, accessed August 1, 2014, www.wpi.edu/academics/library/history/seventyyears/page161.html.

10. Letter to Mr. A. D. Butterfield, Boynton Hall, WPI Worcester, MA from Harry W. Smith, North Grafton, MA, August 5, 1933, in Worcester Polytechnic Institute archives.

11. Washburn, *The Smith's Barn*, 12.

12. George Crompton, *The Crompton Loom* (Worcester, MA, 1949), 25.

13. Washburn, *The Smith's Barn*, 22–23.

14. Letter to Mr. Charles Baker, Secretary Alumni Association of the Worcester Polytechnic Institute (WPI), Worcester, MA, in WPI archives.

15. *Worcester Spy*, "A Sad Suicide," March 5, 1883.

16. Massachusetts Vital Records, 1859. This record was supplied to the author by Kerry Glass, Lincoln, MA.

17. Washburn, *The Smith's Barn*, 10.

18. Typescript in Harry Worcester Smith Archives, National Sporting Library and Museum.

19. Abstract, Crompton and Knowles Loom Works Collection Abstract, Worcester Polytechnic Institute, www.wpi.edu/Images/CMS/Library/MS20_Crompton_Knowles.PDF.

20. Copy of Patent for one of Smith's inventions can be seen at pdfpiw.uspto.gov/.piw?docid=01107553&SectionNum=1&IDKey=42AC35E26352&HomeUrl=http://patft.uspto.gov/netacgi/nph-Parser?Sect2=PTO1%2526Sect2=HITOFF%2526p=1%2526u=/netahtml/PTO/search-bool.html%2526r=1%2526f=G%2526l=50%2526d=PALL%2526S1=1107553.PN.%2526OS=PN/1107553%2526RS=PN/1107553, accessed September 2, 2014. (Note that this patent is registered under Harry Witter Smith. In 1905, when the patent was applied for, he had not yet changed his name to Worcester.)

21. Washburn, *The Smith's Barn*, 94.

22. Allen Potts, *Fox Hunting in America* (Washington: Carnahan Press, ca.1911), 7.

23. Washburn, *The Smith's Barn*, 89.

24. Ibid., 93.

25. "Ting-a-ling" was later immortalized in David Gray's story by that name published in *Gallops* 2 (New York: Derrydale Press, 1929).

26. Washburn, *The Smith's Barn*, 93.

27. George Crompton, *Mariemont* (Worcester, MA: [s.n.], 1952), 15.

28. November 24, 1941 correspondence between Harry Worcester Smith and Jan Blan Van Urk, author of *The Story of American Foxhunting: From Challenge to Full Cry*. Harry Worcester Smith Archives, National Sporting Library and Museum.

29. Harry Worcester Smith, "Making the Grafton Hounds," typed manuscript, ca. 1910, Harry Worcester Smith Archives, National Sporting Library and Museum.

Chapter 6

1. Allen Potts, author of the *Richmond Times Dispatch* articles from which these depictions of each day of The Match come, did not specify if this was "Tadd" Roosevelt, age twenty-six in 1905, or his father "Rosey," aged fifty-one in 1905.

2. Potts's reports from each day of the match can be found in Alexander Mackay-Smith, Appendix B, *The American Foxhound 1747–1967* (Millwood, VA: American Foxhound Club, 1968), 309.

Chapter 7

1. John H. Daniels, "A. Henry Higginson's Unpublished Manuscript" in *National Sporting Library Newsletter*, May 1982, 3–4.

2. Philip K. Crowe, *Sport Is Where You Find It* (New York: Van Nostrand), 145.

3. Alexander Henry Higginson, *An Old Sportsman's Memories 1876–1951* (Berryville, VA: Blue Ridge Press, 1951), 71.

4. Francis Higginson, *New Englands Plantation; Or a Short and True Description of the Commodities and Discommodities of That Country, Written by a Reverend Diuine Now There Resident*, http://books.google.com/books?id=Hf9xAAAAMAAJ&printsec=titlepage#v=onepage&q&f=false; John Higginson, "An Attestation to this Church History of New England" to *Magnalia Chirsti Americana; or the Ecclesiastical History of New England* by Cotton Mather, D.D., F.R.S., , accessed September 15, 2014, http://books.google.com/books?id=49JdS7NoSawC&printsec=frontcover&dq=Magnalia+Christi+Americana#v=onepage&q=Magnalia%20Christi%20Americana&f=false.

5. Bliss Perry, *Life and Letters of Henry Lee Higginson* (Boston: Atlantic Monthly Press, 1921), 2.

6. Kristin Buckstad, "Ann Dolliver: Salem Witch Trials in History and Literature," an Undergraduate Course at UVA, 2001, Salem Witch Trials Documentary Archive and Transcription Project, accessed September 22, 2014, http://salem.lib.virginia.edu/people?group.num=all&mbio.num=mb8.

7. Perry, *Life and Letters of Henry Lee Higginson*, 4. *The Writings of Laco*, nine essays against John Hancock, were written by Stephen Higginson and published in the *Massachusetts Centinel* [sic] in February 17th and March 29th of 1789 (http://csac.history.wisc.edu/ma_writings_of_laco.pdf).

8. Perry, *Life and Letters of Henry Lee Higginson*, 5.

9. Horowitz, *Moral Fire*, 10.

10. Perry, *Life and Letters of Henry Lee Higginson*, 5.

11. Brenda Wineapple, *White Heat: The Friendship of Emily Dickenson and Thomas Wentworth Higginson* (New York: Anchor Books, 2008), 17.

12. Billy Collins, Preface to *The Selected Poems of Emily Dickenson* (New York: The Modern Library, 2000), ix.

13. Perry, *Life and Letters of Henry Lee Higginson*, 22.
14. Ibid., 25.
15. Horowitz, *Moral Fire*, 5, 23.
16. Ibid.
17. Ibid.
18. Perry, *Life and Letters of Henry Lee Higginson*, 179.
19. Ibid., 14.
20. Ibid., 159.
21. Ibid., 191.
22. Ibid., 196.
23. Emma Forbes Cary, *Memories of Fifty Years in the Last Century Written for Her Grandchildren by Caroline Gardiner Curtis and A Sketch of Mrs. Louis Agassiz.* (Boston: privately printed, 1947), 119.
24. Ibid., 122.
25. George Russell Agassiz, ed. *Letters and Recollections of Alexander Agassiz with a Sketch of His Life and Work; Much Material for Early Pages Contributed by Mrs. H. L. Higginson* (Cambridge: Houghton Mifflin/Riverside Press, 1913), 5.
26. Cary, *Memories of Fifty Years*, 125.
27. W. E. B. DuBois, "Of Sons of Masters and Man," in *Writings*, ed. Nathan Huggins (New York: Library of America), 148.
28. Horowitz, *Moral Fire*, 31.
29. Perry, *Life and Letters of Henry Lee Higginson*, 271.
30. Ibid., 51.
31. Ibid., 286.
32. A. H. Higginson, *An Old Sportsman's Memories*, 48.

Chapter 8

1. To sample huntsmen's horn sounds, go to www.foxhuntinglife.com/downloads/378-fhl-downloads.

Chapter 9

1. Held at National Sporting Library and Museum, Middleburg, VA.
2. Richard Henry Spencer, "Hon. Daniel Dulany, 1722–1797 (The Younger)," *Maryland Historical Magazine*, ed. William Hand Browne and Louis Henry Dielman, XIII, no. 1 (March, 1918): 143–160. Accessed October 21, 2014: http://books.google.com/books?id=d_sMAAAAYAAJ&dq=benjamin+tasker+dulany&source=gbs_navlinks_s.
3. Margaret Ann Vogtsberger, *The Dulanys of Welbourne: A Family in Mosby's Confederacy* (Berryville, VA: Rockbridge Publishing Co., ca.1995), xv.
4. Henry James, *Collected Travel Writings: Great Britain and America. English Hours,*

The American Scene, Other Travels (New York: Library of America, 1993), 657.

5. James, *Travels*, 659.

6. Eugene Scheel, *The History of Middleburg and Vicinity* (Warrenton, VA: Piedmont Press, 1987), 101.

7. A visiting fellow at the National Sporting Library and Museum from Leicester University in England once told me that Middleburg was more English than most English villages.

8. Kevin Grigsby, *Howardsville: The Journey of an African-American Community in Loudoun County, Virginia* (self-published, 2008), 480.

9. Vogtsberger, *The Dulanys of Welbourne*, 279.

10. Scheel, *Middleburg and Vicinity*, 91.

11. Allen Potts, "The Hound Trials Start Off Today," *Richmond Times Dispatch*, Wednesday, November 1, 1905, 5.

Chapter 11

1. William Somervile, *The Chase* (London: George Redway, 1735), 2.

2. Ibid., xiv.

3. Captain Lionel Dawson, *Sport in War* (London: Collins, 1936), 50.

4. Ibid., 63.

5. Rt. Honorable Earl of Minto, introduction to *Pink and Scarlet or Hunting as a School for Soldering* [*sic*] by Major General E. A. H. Alderson. (London: W. Heinemann, 1900), xiii.

6. Ibid.

7. David Gilmour, "The Curse of Afghanistan," review of *Return of a King: The Battle for Afghanistan, 1839–42*, by William Dalrymple, *New York Review of Books*, November 21, 2013, www.nybooks.com/articles/archives/2013/nov/21/curse-afghanistan/, 64.

8. Dawson, *Sport in War*, 16.

9. Ibid.

10. Turner Ashby, Commander of the 7th Virginia Calvary under Stonewall Jackson, was a foxhunter from Fauquier County, VA, who took part in the famous eight-hour hunt for the white-tailed fox known as "Old Whitey" before the war in 1845. See Alexander Mackay-Smith, *American Foxhunting Stories* (Millwood, VA: Millwood House, 1996), 62–65.

11. Leo Tolstoy, *War and Peace*, trans. Louise and Aylmer Maude (Oxford: Oxford University Press, 2010), 700.

12. Siegfried Sassoon, *The Complete Memoirs of George Sherston* (London: Farber and Farber, 1972), 136.

13. Ibid., 635.

14. Higginson, *Try Back*, 14.

Chapter 13

1. Frank Townend Barton, *Hounds* (London: J. Long, 1913), 76.

2. David Allan Feller, "Darwin the Dog Lover," www.forbes.com/2009/02/05/ dogs-hunting-cambridge-university-opinions-darwin09_0205_david_allen_ feller.html.

3. Joe Palca, "Dogs Likely Descended from Middle Eastern Wolf," March 18, 2010, www.npr.org/templates/story/story.php?storyId=124768140.

4. Knightley William Horlock [pseud. Scrutator], *The Science of Foxhunting and Management of the Kennel* (London: Routledge, 1868), 5.

5. Jane Ridley, *Foxhunting* (London: William Collins Sons & Co. Ltd., 1990), 17.

6. Van Urk, *The Story of American Foxhunting*, 2:17.

7. Lord Henry William Scott-Bentinck, *The Late Lord Bentinck on Foxhounds: Goodall's Practice* (London: Vinton & Company, 1871), 11.

8. Daphne Moore, *Foxhounds* (London: Batsford, 1981), 16.

9. Charles Darwin, *The Origin of Species; by Means of Natural Selection of the Preservation of Favoured Races in the Struggle for Life* (New York: Signet Classics, Penguin Group, 2003), 29.

10. Ridley, *Foxhunting*, 134.

11. Frank Sherman Peer, *The Hunting Field with Horse and Hound* (New York: Mitchell Kennerley, 1910), 141.

12. Cuthbert Bradley, *Hunting Reminiscences of Frank Gillard (Huntsman): With the Belvoir Hounds 1860–1896* (London: E. Arnold, 1898), 180.

13. Higginson, *Try Back*, 7.

14. Ibid., 8.

15. Ibid., 7.

16. Woods Walker, *Walker Hounds: Their Origin and Development* (Cynthiana, KY: Hobson Book Press, 1945), 4.

17. Bob Lee Maddox, *History of the Walker Hound, 1961*, in *The American Foxhound: 1747–1967*, ed. Alexander Mackay-Smith (Millwood, VA: The American Foxhound Club, 1968), 32.

18. Ibid.

19. Albin S. Payne [pseud. "Nicholas Spicer"], "Great Run and the Last of Old Whitey (1845), originally published in *Turf, Field and Farm*, Dec. 26, 1884, in *The American Foxhound: 1747–1967*, by Alexander Mackay-Smith (Millwood, VA: The American Foxhound Club, 1968), 58–61.

20. Van Urk, *The Story of American Foxhunting*, 1:217.

21. Harry Worcester Smith, excerpt of unpublished biography, in *The American Foxhound: 1747–1967*, ed. Alexander Mackay-Smith (Millwood, VA: The American Foxhound Club, 1968), 94.

22. Ibid.

23. Harry Worcester Smith, "Harry Worcester Smith, The Grafton Hounds, and the 1905 Hound Match," in *The American Foxhound: 1747–1967*, ed. Alexander Mackay-Smith, 105.

24. Mackay-Smith, *The American Foxhound*, 9.

25. Walker, *Walker Hounds*, 10.

26. Mackay-Smith, *The American Foxhound*, 87.

27. Worcester Smith, "Harry Worcester Smith, The Grafton Hounds, and the 1905 Hound Match," 104–8.

28. Ibid.

29. Burrell Frank Bywaters, "Burrell Frank Bywaters," in *The American Foxhound: 1747–1967*, 86.

Chapter 15

1. John Welcome, *The Sporting Empress: The Story of Elizabeth of Austria and Bay Middleton* (London: Joseph, 1985), 54.

2. Ibid., 15.

3. Ibid., 34.

4. Ibid.

5. An English judge at a summer show at Foxcroft School in Middleburg once said to me, "My dear, you *look* better than you *are*."

6. Bell Beach, *Riding and Driving for Women* (London: T. Werner Laurie, Ltd, 1912), 58.

7. George F. Underhill, *A Century of English Foxhunting* (London: R.A. Everett & Co., 1900), 293.

8. R. S. Surtees, "Mr. Sponge's Sporting Tour," in *The Fox-Hunter's Bedside Book* compiled by The Lady Apsley, M.F.H. (New York: Charles Scribner's Sons, 1949), 528.

9. Alice M. Hayes, *The Horsewoman: A Practical Guide to Side-Saddle Riding*, ed. M. Horace Hayes (London: Hurst and Blackett, 1903), 1.

10. See http://en.wikipedia.org/wiki/Sidesaddle#mediaviewer/File:STACE-Esther_M.jpg, accessed October 19, 2014.

11. Mrs. Amy Charlotte Bewickle Menzies's hilarious book, *Women in the Hunting Field* (London: Vinton, 1913), 15.

Chapter 16

1. See Peter Nova, "Dogs' dazzling sense of smell," www.pbs.org/wgbh/nova/nature/dogs-sense-of-smell.htm.

2. *National Geographic*, "How the Nose Knows," in "The Dogs of War," June 2014.

3. Ronald Tree, foreword to *The Huntsman at the Gate* by Amet Jenks (Philadelphia: J. B. Lippincott, 1952), 6.

4. Tolstoy, *War and Peace*, 527–28. Book two, part four, chapters three through five describe one of the greatest hunting scenes in literature.

5. George Lawrence Forsyth ("Larry") Birdsong, "The Red Fox," in *American Foxhunting Stories*, ed. Alexander Mackay-Smith (Millwood, VA: Millwood House, 1996), 57.

6. P. C. Spink, "Some New Thoughts on Hunting Scent," in *Hounds* 2, no. 6 (October 1986): 18–19.

7. Redmond Stewart, "What Makes Scent Good?" *The Chronicle of the Horse*, Friday, September 30, 1988, 14–15.

8. Henry W. Hooker, MFH, "Remarks on Scent," *Covertside: A Publication of the Masters of Foxhound Association*, 1:2, 4–5.

9. See Peter Beckford and William Somervile for two of the oldest and most respected texts on hunting.

10. Birdsong, "The Red Fox," 56–62.

11. Stewart, "What Makes Scent Good?" 14.

12. Joseph B. Thomas, "Scent," in *The Chronicle of the Horse*, October 1988, 90.

13. H. M. Budgett, *Hunting by Scent* (London: Eyre and Spottiswoode, 1933), 20–26.

14. Henry Tegner in *'Horse and Hound' Foxhunting Companion*, selected and introduced by "Foxford"; foreword by The Duke of Beaufort (Feltham: Country Life Books, 1978), 167–70.

15. Spink, "Some New Thoughts on Hunting Scent," 19.

16. P. Quignon, E. Kirkness, E. Cadieu, N. Touleimat, R. Guyon, C. Renier, C. Hitte, C. André, C. Fraser, and F. Galibert, "Comparison of the canine and human olfactory receptor gene repertoires." www.ncbi.nlm.nih.gov/pubmed/14659017. Accessed 3/27/14. A shy person signing his or her name as "H. F." in *Hounds* (September 30, 1988) reports that "the mucous membrane in a hound's nose devoted to the detection and appreciation of smell is equal in extent to half the body surface, whereas in man it is scarcely larger than a postage stamp." H. F. doesn't mention where he gets his information, but more recent research finds that a dog has over twelve hundred olfactory receptors compared to a human's measly eight hundred.

17. Durham, J.M.M.B., and Richardson, R.J. *Melton and Homespun: Nature and Sport in Prose and Verse*. London: Chapman and Hall, Ltd., 1913. Accessed July 13, 2015: https://books.google.com/books?id=9klDAAAAIAAJ&pg=PA19&lpg=PA19&dq=old+blue+pye&source=bl&ots=hu0oi-R28A&sig=MTKAUBOZDPGMlumfI5ovq8MYjRQ&hl=en&sa=X&ved=0CDkQ6AEwCGoVChMIp-aK6l7PYxgIVwWg-Ch2HcAm2#v=onepage&q=old%20blue%20pye&f=false "Old Blue Pye. "The Old Blue Pye" is an old hunting song reprinted in many texts containing such poetry and prose oral history.

18. Payne, "Great Run and the Last of Old Whitey (1845)," in Mackay-Smith's *The American Foxhound* (1968), 58–61.

19. Kenneth Varty, Introduction to *Reynard the Fox; a Study of the Fox in Medieval English Art* (Leicester: Leicester University Press, 1967), 21–24.

20. Ibid., 21.

21. A. Scott Berg, *Max Perkins: Editor of Genius* (London: Pan Books, 1999), 363.

22. Van Urk, *The Story of American Foxhunting: From Challenge to Full Cry, vol. 1* (New York: Derrydale Press, ca. 1940–1941), 5.

23. Hooker, *Remarks on Scent*, 4.

Chapter 19

1. Payne, "Great Run and the Last of Old Whitey (1845)," in Mackay-Smith's *The American Foxhound* (1968), 58–61.

2. Ayrshire is now owned by Sandy Lerner, cofounder of Cisco Systems, who operates it as a certified organic farm.

3. "Jericho Turnpike; The Great Hunts of Virginia," *Fortune*, November 1930, 53.

4. Ibid., 51.

5. Ibid.

6. Alexander Henry Higginson and Julian Ingersoll Chamberlain, *Hunts of the United States and Canada; Their Masters, Hounds and Histories* (Boston: F. L. Wills, 1908), 81.

7. Ibid., 86.

8. Ibid., 115.

9. Daphne Moore, *The Book of Foxhounds* (London: J. A. Aulen & Co., 1964), 36.

10. Harry Worcester Smith Archives, National Sporting Library and Museum, Middleburg, VA.

11. Ibid.

12. Ibid.

13. A. H. Higginson, *An Old Sportsman's Memories*, 93.

14. Smith Archives, NSLM.

15. Higginson, *Try Back*, 19.

16. Ibid., 98.

17. Ibid.

18. A. H. Higginson, *An Old Sportsman's Memories*, 95.

19. Ibid., 106.

20. Ibid., 109.

21. Harry Worcester Smith, *The Pulse of the People* (self-published, Lordvale: Worcester, MA, Spring 1919), held at the American Antiquarian Society, Worcester, MA.

22. J. N. P. Watson, *British & Irish Hunts & Huntsmen*, vol. 2 (London: B. T. Batsford, 1982), 146.

23. Smith Archives, NSLM.

24. *The Chronicle*, "A Personage of the Chase," March 5, 1943, 7.

25. Martha Wolfe, "Edward Troye and his Biographers; The Archives of Harry Worcester Smith and Alexander Mackay-Smith" in *Coming Home Series; Edward Troye (1808–1874)* catalogue for the Edward Troye exhibit "Faithfulness to Nature: Paintings by Edward Troye" at the National Sporting Library and Museum, October 26, 2014–March 29, 2015, 17.

26. Ibid., 21.

27. Ibid., 20.

28. Smith Archives.

29. Alexander Henry Higginson Collection, London Library, England.

30. National Sporting Library and Museum Newsletter, Winter 1996.

31. A. H. Higginson, *An Old Sportsman's Memories*, 95.

32. The envelope is framed and held in the Harry Worcester Smith archives at the National Sporting Library and Museum in Middleburg, VA.

BIBLIOGRAPHY

Agassiz, George Russell, ed. *Letters and Recollections of Alexander Agassiz with a Sketch of His Life and Work: Much Material for Early Pages Contributed by Mrs. H. L. Higginson.* Cambridge: Houghton Mifflin/Riverside Press, 1913.

Apsley, The Lady. *The Fox-Hunter's Bedside Book.* New York: Charles Scribner's Sons, 1949.

Barton, Frank Townend. *Hounds.* London: J. Long, 1913.

Beach, Bell. *Riding and Driving for Women.* London: T. Werner Laurie, Ltd., 1912.

Beckford, Peter. *Thoughts on Hunting, in a Series of Familiar Letters to a Friend.* London, Cowie, Jolland and Co., 1840. Copied electronically by General Books. www.General-Books.net.

Bentinck, Lord Henry William. *The Late Lord Bentinck on Foxhounds; Goodall's Practice.* London: Vinton & Company, 1871.

Berg, Scott. A. *Max Perkins: Editor of Genius.* London: Pan Books, 1999.

Birdsong, L. F. "The Red Fox" in *Sporting Sketches from 'The Countryman', 1863–1864.* Atlanta: Emery University, 1955.

Bradley, Cuthbert. *Hunting Reminiscences of Frank Gillard (huntsman): with the Belvoir Hounds 1860–1896.* London: E. Arnold, 1898.

Buckstad, Kristin, "Ann Dolliver; Salem Witch Trials in History and Literature, an Undergraduate Course at UVA, 2001." Salem Witch Trials Documentary Archive and Transcription Project. Accessed September 22, 2014. http://salem.lib.virginia.edu/people?group .num=all&mbio.num=mb8.

Budgett, H. M. *Hunting by Scent.* London: Eyre and Spottiswoode, 1933.

Bywaters, Burrell Frank. "Burrell Frank Bywaters." In *The American Foxhound: 1747–1967,* by Alexander Mackay-Smith (Millwood, VA: The American Foxhound Club, 1968).

Cary, Emma Forbes. *Memories of Fifty Years in the Last Century Written for Her Grandchildren by Caroline Gardiner Curtis and A Sketch of Mrs. Louis Agassiz.* Boston: privately printed, 1947.

The Chronicle, "A Personage of the Chase," March 5, 1943.

Collins, Billy. *The Selected Poems of Emily Dickinson*. New York: The Modern Library, 2000.

Crompton, George. *The Crompton Loom*. Self-published. Worcester, MA: 1949.

———. *Mariemont*. Worcester, MA: [s.n.], 1952.

Crowe, Philip K. *Sport Is Where You Find It*. New York: D. Van Nostroud Co., Inc., 1953.

Daniels, John H. "A. Henry Higginson's Unpublished Manuscript" in *National Sporting Library Newsletter*, May 1982, 3–4.

Darwin, Charles. *The Origin of Species; by Means of Natural Selection of The Preservation of Favoured Races in the Struggle for Life*. New York: Signet Classics, Penguin Group, 2003.

Dawson, Lionel. *Sport in War*. New York: Charles Scribner's Sons, 1937.

Du Bois, W.E.B. "Of Sons and Masters and Man." In *Writings*, ed. Nathan Huggins. New York: Library of America, 1986.

Durham, J.M.M.B., and Richardson, R.J. *Melton and Homespun: Nature and Sport in Prose and Verse*. London: Chapman and Hall, Ltd., 1913. Accessed July 13, 2015. https://books.google.com/books?id=9klDAAAAIAAJ&pg=PA19&lpg=PA19&dq=old+blue+pye&source=bl&ots=hu0oi-R28A&sig=MTKAUBOZDPGMlumfI5ovq8MYjRQ&hl=en&sa=X&ved=0CDkQ6AEwCGoVChMIpaK6l7PYxgIVwWg-Ch2HcAm2#v=onepage&q=old%20blue%20pye&f=false

Elliot, Samuel Aikens, ed. *Bibliographical History of Massachusetts; Biographies and Autobiographies of the Leading Men in the State*, Vol. III. Boston: Massachusetts Biographical Society, 1911.

Everdell, William. "Space-Time Cubism." *New York Times*, May, 6, 2001. Accessed May 20. 2014. http://nytimes.com/books/01/05/06/reviews/010506.06everdet.html.

Feller, David Allan. "Darwin the Dog Lover," forbes.com, February 5, 2009. Accessed March 3, 2014. www.forbes.com/2009/02/25/dogs-hunting-cambridge-university-opinions-darwin09_0205_david_allen_fuller.html.

Forbes, A., and Green, J. W. *The Rich Men of Massachusetts: Containing the Reputed Wealth of About Fifteen Hundred Persons, with Brief Sketches of More Than A Thousand Characters*. Boston: W. V. Spencer, 1851. Accessed August 26, 2013. plymouthcolony.net/resources/richmen/001.html.

Foxford (Henry Tegner) in *'Horse and Hound' Foxhunting Companion, Selected and Introduced by Foxford, Forward by The Duke of Beaufort.* Feltham: Country Life Books, 1978.

Gilmour, David. "The Curse of Afghanistan." Review of *Return of a King; the Battle for Afghanistan, 1839–42,* by William Dalrymple. *New York Review of Books,* November 21, 2013. www.nybooks.com/articles/archives/2013/nov/21/curse-afghanistan/.

Grafton, Anthony, Glenn W. Most, and Salvatore Settis. *The Classical Tradition.* Cambridge, MA: The Belknap Press of Harvard University Press, 2013.

Graham, Joseph A. *The Sporting Dog.* New York: The Macmillan Company, 1904.

Green, Brian. "One Hundred Years of Uncertainty." NYtimes.com, April 8, 2005. Accessed May 20, 2014. www.nytimes.com/2005/04/08/opinion/08greene.html/.

Grigsby, Kevin. *Howardsville; The Journey of an African-American Community in Loudoun County, Virginia.* Self-published, 2008.

Hayes, Alice M., ed. M. Horace Hayes. *The Horsewoman; A Practical Guide to Side-Saddle Riding.* London: Hurst and Blackett, 1903.

Higginson, Alexander Henry, and Julian Ingersoll Chamberlain, *Hunts of the United States and Canada; Their Masters, Hounds and Histories.* Boston: F. L. Wills, 1908.

Higginson, Alexander Henry. *Try Back; A Huntsman's Reminiscences.* New York: Huntington Press, 1931.

———. *An Old Sportsman's Memories 1876–1951.* Berryville, VA: Blue Ridge Press, 1951.

Higginson, Francis. *New Englands Plantation; Or a Short and True Description of the Commodities and Discommodities of That Country, Written by a Reverend Diuine Now There Resident.* London: Printed by T.C. and R.C. for Michael Sparke, dwelling at the Blue Bible in Greene Arbor in the little Old Bailey, 1680. Accessed September 15, 2014. http://books.google.com/books?id=Hf9xAAAAMAAJ&printsec=titlepage#v=onepage&q&f=false

Higginson, John. "An Attestation to this Church History of New England" to *Magnalia Chirsti Americana; or the Ecclesiastical History of New England* by Cotton Mather, D.D., F.R.S. http://books.google.com/books?id=49JdS7NoSawC&printsec=frontcover&dq=Magn

alia+Christi+Americana#v=onepage&q=Magnalia%20Christi%20
Americana&f=false.

History.com. *Albert Einstein.* A&E Network. 2009. Accessed
March 6, 2014. www.history.com/topics/albert-einstein/
videos#beyond-the-big-bang-albert-einstein.

Hooker, Henry W., MFH. "Remarks on Scent," *Covertside: A Publication
of the Masters of Foxhound Association,* 1:2, 1–5.

Horlock, K. W. *The Science of Foxhunting and Management of the Kennel,
by Scrutator [pseud.]* London: George Rutledge & Sons, 1868.

Horne, Philip. "James, Henry (1843–1916)." *Oxford Dictionary of
National Biography.* Accessed March 7, 2014. www.oxforddnb.com/
view/article/34150.

Horowitz, Joseph. *Moral Fire: Musical Portraits from America's Fin-de-
Siecle.* Berkeley, CA: University of California Press, 2012.

Howard, Don A. "Albert Einstein as a Philosopher of Science," *Physics
Today* 58(12), 34 (2005); doi: 10.1063/1.2169442. http://dx.doi
.org/10.1063/1.2169442.

"H. R." "Thoughts on Scent." *Hounds.* September, 1992, p. 22.

Hughes, Stuart H. *Consciousness and Society.* New Brunswick (U.S.A.):
Transaction Publishers, 2008.

James, Henry. *Henry James: Collected Travel Writings, Great Britain and
America: English Hours/The American Scene/Other Travels.* New York:
Library of America, 1993.

James, William. "Pragmatism: A New Name for Some Old Ways of
Thinking." In *Writings 1902–1910.* New York: Literary Classics of
the United States, Inc., 1987.

———. *The Varieties of Religious Experience: A Study in Human Nature.*
New York: Literary Classics of the United States, Inc., 1987.

"Jericho Turnpike; The Great Hunts of Virginia," *Fortune,* November
1930, 53.

Kaminski, John P., Gaspore J. Salandino, Richard Leffler, Charles H.
Schoenleber, and Margaret A. Hogan. "The Documentary History
of the Ratification of the Constitution Digital Edition." Charlot-
tesville: University of Virginia Press, 2009. Accessed September 15,
2014: http://csac.history.wisc.edu/ma_writings_of_laco.pdf.

Kloss, William, and Doreen Bolger. *Art in the White House: A Nation's
Pride.* Washington, D.C.: The White House Historical Association
in cooperation with the National Geographic Society, 1992. www
.whitehouseresearch.org/assetbank-whha/action/viewAsset?id=134.

Krystal, Arthur. "The Age of Reason." *The New Yorker,* October 22, 2007, 94–103, http://www.newyorker.com/magazine/2007/10/22/age-of-reason-2.

Lears, Jackson. *Rebirth of a Nation: The Making of Modern America, 1877–1920.* New York: HarperCollins Publishers, 2009.

Mackay-Smith, Alexander. *The American Foxhound: 1747–1967.* Millwood, VA: The American Foxhound Club, 1968.

———. *American Foxhunting Stories.* Millwood, VA: Millwood House, 1996.

Maddox, Bob Lee. "History of the Walker Hound, 1961" in *The American Foxhound: 1747–1967* by Alexander Mackay-Smith. Millwood, VA: The American Foxhound Club, 1968.

Magee, Glenn Alexander. *The Hegel Dictionary.* New York: Continuum International Publishing Group, 2010.

Menzies, Mrs. Amy Charlotte Bewickle. *Women in the Hunting Field.* London: Vinton, 1913.

Miller, Arthur I. *Einstein/Picasso: Space, Time, and the Beauty That Causes Havoc.* New York: Basic Books, 2001.

Minto, Rt. Honorable Earl of. Introduction to *Pink and Scarlet or Hunting as a School for Soldering* [*sic*], by Alderson, Edwin Alfred Hervey, xiii. London: W. Heinemann, 1900.

Moore, Daphne. *Foxhound.* London: Batsford, 1981.

New York Times. "Dr. Albert Einstein Dies in Sleep at 76; World Mourns Loss of Great Scientist," April 19, 1955. www.nytimes.com/learning/general/onthisday/bday/0314.html.

Nova, Peter. "Dogs' Dazzling Sense of Smell." http://www.pbs.org/wgbh/nova/nature/dogs-sense-of-smell.htm.

Pais, Abraham. Neils Bohr's Times: *In Physics, Philosophy and Polity.* Oxford: Clarendon Press, 1991.

———. *Subtle Is the Lord: The Science and the Life of Albert Einstein.* Oxford: Oxford University Press, 1982.

Palca, Joe. "Dogs Likely Descended from Lone Wolf," npr.org. www.npr.org/templates/story/story.pho?storyId=124768140.

Paterniti, Michael. "The Dogs of War." *National Geographic,* June, 2014.

Payne, Albin S. [pseud. "Nicholas Spicer"], "Great Run and the Last of Old Whitey (1845), originally published in *Turf, Field, and Farm,* Dec. 26, 1884", in *The American Foxhound: 1747–1967* by Alexander Mackay-Smith (Millwood, VA: The American Foxhound Club, 1968).

Peer, Frank Sherman. *Cross Country with Horse and Hound.* New York: C. Scribner's Sons, 1902.

————. *The Hunting Field with Horse and Hound.* New York: Mitchell Kennerley, 1910.

Perry, Bliss. *Life and Letters of Henry Lee Higginson, Vol. I,* 4. Boston: Atlantic Monthly Press, 1921.

Potts, Allen. "The Hound Trials Start Off Today." *The Richmond Times Dispatch,* Wed., November 1, 1905. Accessed October 21, 2014. http://chroniclingamerica.loc.gov/lccn/sn85038615/1905-11-01/ed-1/seq-1/.

————. *Fox Hunting in America.* Washington: The Carnahan Press, c. 1911.

Quignon, P., E. Kirkness, E. Cadieu, N. Touleimat, R. Guyon, C. Renier, C. Hitte, C. André, C. Fraser, and F. Galibert, "Comparison of the canine and human olfactory receptor gene repertoires." Accessed 3/27/14. www.ncbi.nlm.nih.gov/pubmed/14659017.

Ridley, Jane. *Foxhunting.* London: William Collins Sons & Co. Ltd., 1990.

Rivas, Mim Eichler. *Beautiful Jim Key: The Lost History of a Horse and a Man Who Changed the World.* New York: HarperCollins Publishers, 2005.

Russell, Bertrand. *A History of Western Philosophy.* New York: Simon & Schuster, Inc., 1945.

Santayana, George. *Character & Opinion in the United States; with Reminiscences of William James and Josiah Royce and Academic Life in America.* New York: Charles Scribner's Sons, 1922.

Sassoon, Siegfried. *The Complete Memoirs of George Sherston.* London: Farber and Farber Limited, 1972.

Scheel, Eugene. *The History of Middleburg and Vicinity.* Warrenton, VA: Piedmont Press, 1987.

Schmidt, Barbara. "Mark Twain Quotations, Newspaper Collections and Related Resources." Accessed October 31, 2014. www.twainquotes.com/19351102.html.

Shepard, Gordon M. "The Human Sense of Smell: Are We Better Than We Think?" *PLoS Biol.,* May 2004; 2(5): e146. Published online May 11, 2004. doi: 10.1371/journal.pbio.0020146. Accessed 3/27/14. www.ncbi.nlm.nih.gov/pmc/articles/PMC406401/.

Sloane, William. "Life of Napoleon Bonaparte." *Century Magazine* L (1895) 5: 643–673.

Smith, Harry Worcester. "Making the Grafton Hounds." Typed manuscript, c. 1910. Harry Worcester Smith Archives. National Sporting Library and Museum.

———. *The Pulse of the People*. Self-published, Lordvale: Worcester, MA, USA, Spring 1919. American Antiquarian Society, Worcester, MA.

———. *A Sporting Family of the Old South*. Albany NY: J. B. Lyon Company, 1936.

Smith, Josephine McCurdy Caroline. *A Sketch of Mrs. C. W. Smith's Life Written by Herself, 1909*. Self-published, 1909. Held at the American Antiquarian Society, Worcester, MA.

Somervile, William. *The Chase*. London: W. Boyer, W. Strahan & R. Baldwin, 1767.

Spencer, Richard Henry. "Hon. Daniel Dulany, 1722–1797 (The Younger)," *Maryland Historical Magazine*, ed. William Hand Browne and Louis Henry Dielman XIII, no. 1 (March, 1918): 143–160. Accessed October 21, 2014. http://books.google.com/books?id=d_sMAAAAYAAJ&dq=benjamin+tasker+dulany&source=gbs_navlinks_s.

Spink, P. C. "Some New Thoughts on Hunting Scent." *Hounds*. Vol. 2., No. 6., October 1986.

Stewart, Redmond C. "What Makes Scent Good?" *The Chronicle of the Horse*. September 30, 1988, 14–15.

Taylor, Herbert Foster. *Seventy Years of the Worcester Polytechnic Institute*. Worcester, MA: Worcester Polytechnic Institute. Accessed August 1, 2014. www.wpi.edu/academics/library/history/seventyyears/page161.html.

Tegner, Henry in *'Horse and Hound' Foxhunting Companion*, selected and introduced by "Foxford"; foreword by The Duke of Beaufort. Feltham: Country Life Books, 1978.

Thomas, Joseph B. "Scent." *The Chronicle of the Horse*, October 1988, 90. Taken from *Hounds and Hunting Through the Ages*. Lanham, MD: Derrydale Press. Originally Published, 1928.

Thompson, Kathy. "Red Fox (Vulpes vulpes)." Northern State University, Aberdeen, SD, 1997. Accessed March 11, 2014. /www3.northern.edu/natsource/MAMMALS/Redfox1.htm.

Tolstoy, Leo. *War and Peace*. Translated by Louise and Aylmer Maude. Revised and Edited with an Introduction by Amy Mandelker. Oxford: Oxford University Press, 2010.

Tree, Ronald. Foreword to *The Huntsman at the Gate* by Amet Jenks. Philadelphia: J. B. Lippincott, 1952.

Underhill, George F. *A Century of English Foxhunting*. London: R. A. Everett & Co., 1900.

Van Urk, Jan Blan. *The Story of American Foxhunting: From Challenge to Full Cry*, Vol. 1. New York: Derrydale Press, c. 1940–1941.

Varty, Kenneth. "Introduction." Reyanard the Fox: *A Study of the Fox in Medieval English Art.* Leicester: Leicester University Press, 1967.

Vogtsberger, Margaret Ann. *The Dulanys of Welbourne: A Family in Mosby's Confederacy.* Berryville, VA: Rockbridge Publishing Co., c. 1995.

Walker, Woods. *Walker Hounds: Their Origin and Development.* Cynthiana, KY: The Hobson Book Press, 1945.

Washburn, Robert Morris. *The Smith's Barn; A Child's History of the West Side, Worcester 1880–1923.* Worcester, MA: Exclusive distributors, Davis & Banister, 1923.

Watson, J.N.P. *British and Irish Hunts & Huntsmen, Vol. II.* London: B.T. Batsford, 1982.

Welcome, John. *The Sporting Empress: The Story of Elizabeth of Austria and Bay Middleton.* London: Joseph, 1975.

Whitman, Walt. "Starting from Paumanok." *Leaves of Grass.* www.bartleby.com/142/.

Williams, Dr. Dave. *The History of Loudoun County, Virginia*, "How Loudoun County Got Its Name," originally in *The Blue Ridge Leader.* Accessed July 4, 2014. www.loudounhistory.org/history/loudoun-how-named.htm.

Wineapple, Brenda. *White Heat: The Friendship of Emily Dickinson and Thomas Wentworth Higginson.* New York: Anchor Books, A Division of Random House, Inc., 2008.

Wolfe, Martha. "Edward Troye and his Biographers; The Archives of Harry Worcester Smith and Alexander Mackay-Smith" in *Coming Home Series; Edward Troye (1808–1874)* catalogue for the Edward Troye exhibit "Faithfulness to Nature: Paintings by Edward Troye" at the National Sporting Library and Museum, October 26, 2014–March 29, 2015, 17.

Woods, Joseph E. *The Worcester County West Agricultural Society: A Brief History of the Barre Cattle Shows.* Worcester, MA: The Skelley Print, 1914. Accessed August 26, 2014. https://ia600303.us.archive.org/35/items/briefhistoryofba00wood/briefhistoryofba00wood.pdf.

Index

About the Author

Martha Wolfe holds a Master of Fine Arts in literature and creative writing from The Bennington Writing Seminars at Bennington College. She has twice been a John H. Daniels Fellow at the National Sporting Library in Middleburg, Virginia, where she conducted research for *The Great Hound Match of 1905*. Martha and her husband live on a farm in northwestern Frederick County, Virginia, where they've raised three boys, dozens of family dogs, cats, chickens, a few pigs, a couple of steers, and a small herd of Connemara ponies. Each summer Martha "walks" foxhound puppies for Blue Ridge Hunt.